FOLLOWING HARD AFTER GOD

AUTOBIOGRAPHY OF

J. David Eshleman

PHILIPPIANS 3:10-11

Let the Supernatural Become Natural

Following Hard After God

Autobiography of J. David Eshleman

Library of Congress Number: 2022939737
International Standard Book Number: 978-1-60126-805-1

Published by

Masthof Press

219 Mill Road | Morgantown, PA 19543-9516

www.Masthof.com

THIS BOOK IS DEDICATED
TO OUR FAMILY AND
TO ALL WHO DESIRE TO BE
FULLY DEVOTED FOLLOWERS
OF THE LORD JESUS CHRIST.

"I want to know Christ—yes, to know the power of His resurrection and participation in His sufferings, becoming like Him in His death, and so, somehow, attaining to the resurrection from the dead."

PHILIPPIANS 3:10-11

TABLE OF CONTENTS

PREFACE

In one sense it seems presumptuous to write an autobiography. However, it is clear our lives are designed to help others. The Apostle Paul admonishes us to, "encourage one another and build each other up, just as you are doing." (I Thessalonians 5:11). I have faith to believe these pages will move the reader to a closer walk with the Lord Jesus. Even the opening words of the text: "God chose you before the world was formed," (Ephesians 1:4), will have a positive effect throughout your life if you keep them in focus.

Like David, I made a serious effort "to follow hard after God." (Psalm 63:8 KJV). Jeremiah promises, "You will seek me and find me when you seek me with all your heart." (Jeremiah 29:13).

Thus, I join Luke in saying that, in God, "we live and move and have our being." (Acts 17:28).

May the Lord use my life to encourage others to walk faithfully with Jesus. While the focus is on my life, I know that readers will also be drawn closer to Jesus by Helen, my wife's intimate relationship with Jesus. Without her, this book would not have been written.

As I was writing, I received the following email from our good friends, whom we learned to know 27 years ago when I pastored their church. I pray that Helen's and my life will touch your life as we touched theirs:

> "Merry Christmas and Happy New Year to our dear Helen and Dave.
>
> It is about time I tell you how much you are thought about and lifted in prayer every day! But I need to tell you how much you are regarded, all that I remember from your time with us here.
>
> Picturing your smile, Helen, and believing that God gave you joy, because your body gave you pain. Talking to people

that you, Dave, went door to door to share the love of Christ. ... Visiting your home in Laurel, in Pennsylvania and in Ohio and soaking up time with you as we shared family stories. Sitting in so many living rooms of church families as we sang and shared Bible passages, you have both saturated this area with your influence.

You identified that Cottage City Mennonite Church had outgrown the walls of the building on Forty-Second Ave. You helped us transition into a church with many nations represented. Dave, you led with humility. Helen, you led with humor and strength.

I love you both and pray that God gives you rest at night and allows you, Helen, to sleep because of physical pain. I pray that you know, Dave, how much our Lord smiles when He looks at you. Your love of Christ is a lesson I draw on regularly. Thank you both for using your everything for sharing Jesus. I love you. We love you.

God bless you,

José and Anne"

Many illustrations include individuals who are still living. I have changed the names of a few to protect their identity.

All Scripture quotations, unless otherwise indicated, are taken from the New International Version. This autobiography takes the liberty to incorporate nearly 250 Scriptures. Most of these are referenced and also printed. Hopefully this will help the reader to store up God's word in their heart. (Psalm 119:11).

INNOCENTS AND FORMATION

1936-1942

See yourselves as God sees you. The Apostle Paul wrote: "God chose us (you) in Him before the creation of the world." (Ephesians 1:4). Can you imagine a better way to begin your life? Meditating on the fact that God had His eye on you before He created the world. If you are conscious of that truth it will affect how you live each day.

Two Necessary Births

In John 3:3, Jesus said, "Very truly I tell you, no one can see the kingdom of God unless they are born again."

What does it mean to be born again? Jesus said, "This is eternal life: that they know you, the only true God, and Jesus Christ, whom you have sent." (John 17:3). The important thing is to know Jesus, not just know about Him but let Him live His life through you.

I've been asked different times if we need to know the date we were born again to be saved. My answer is: "I know I was born but I don't remember being present on Sunday morning November 15, 1936, when I was born. I know I am a child of God because I invited Jesus to take over my life, my body, soul and spirit. I experience His supernatural leading continually."

Indeed, God "rescued us from the dominion of darkness and brought us into the kingdom of the Son He loves, in whom we have redemption, the forgiveness of sins." (Colossians 1:13-14). It is not necessary to know the date you were born into God's family.

My First Home

From birth I lived in the house my mother's father, Grandpa Graver, built along the main street in Conestoga Center, Pennsylvania, where it stands today. I never met Grandpa Graver, since he died 10 years before I was born. The house is easy to spot, with white pillars on the front porch.

After being away for 75 years, I had the privilege of being invited inside. I was amazed at the smallness of the house. Today we have smaller families with houses three times the square footage as those in pre-World War II days. Because of the "necessity" for each child to have his own room, we have greatly limited our ability to give generously to God's mission in the world.

The Great Depression

Even though the Great Depression was officially over before I was born, our family felt its effects. Dad frequently said how thankful he was to have work. Earlier, he had worked for a farmer who paid him one dollar a day plus lunch. Later, the farmer added an additional quarter to his day's wages. As a young boy at Christmas, he received an orange and a few nuts as his Christmas present.

Grandpa Graver's property included a small barn, still standing, where we kept a few chickens that supplied us with eggs. A large vegetable garden with a row of raspberries supplemented many healthy meals, aiding the family budget.

By the time I was born in 1936, Dad was driving truck for Lancaster County Public Works—mainly carrying stone in summer and plowing snow in the winter. He often talked about the truck having poor brakes, especially in winter when the brakes froze up. He had us sitting on the edge of our chairs as he shared dangerous stories about nearly losing his life because of those brakes.

One of my first memories was the weekly ice truck, and the "ice man" who placed large blocks of ice in our ice refrigerator. We purchased our milk from a local dairy farmer.

Siblings

I had two siblings: Faith is six years older than me. Miriam was born three years before me but lived only one day. Her death was extremely difficult for Mother. She seemed to internalize the pain of Miriam's death. We seldom talked about her short life. When I was born, Faith was disappointed because she wanted a little sister. When I was on the way, Faith was not permitted to tell her schoolmates she was anticipating the birth of a sister or brother. Because of Miriam's death, Mother feared I would not live.

What a joy it will be for me to have Miriam welcome me in heaven. Jesus said, "Let the little children come to me, and do not hinder them, for the kingdom of heaven belongs to such as these." (Matthew 19:14).

In Ezekiel 16:21, God refers to children as "my children." He even seems to assign angels to children. Jesus said, "See that you do not despise one of these little ones. For I tell you that their angels in heaven always see the face of my Father in heaven." (Matthew 18:10).

Sundays Were Special

As I was growing up, life was regimented, but Sundays were special. Without question, we attended church. River Corner Mennonite Church, Mother's home church, lay 3 miles southwest of our home. The first building was built in 1760 and the present building in 1882.

When I was an infant, Sunday school started at 9 a.m. in this quaint, old stone building, followed by worship at 10 a.m.

Many Mennonites emigrated from Europe in the 18th century. My great, great-grandfather Johannes Eschellman, emigrated from Germany. He arrived in Philadelphia on the *von Rotterdam* on September 11, 1731. The Graver family emigrated from Switzerland about the same time. Mennonites had been persecuted in Europe because they would not participate in war. To avoid persecution, they left for America.

I was in the "card class," with a few other preschool children. Each Sunday we received a postcard-sized card containing a Bible picture on one side and a Bible story on the other, which our teacher would read to us.

All the Sunday school classes met in the main auditorium, with no dividers between classes. During the church service I sat with Dad. He often kept pink or white lozenge candy in his pocket, which I enjoyed. (I much preferred the pink ones over the white peppermint candies, because those were too "bitey.") The men sat on one side of the church and the women on the other. Years later this tradition gradually changed, and the men and women were free to sit together.

Following the service, people intermingled: leisurely talking and catching up on the local news. Frequently, we either invited a family home for lunch (called "dinner") or they invited us to their home. These were times for making lasting friendships.

An Exciting Revitalization

River Corner Church was slowly declining over the past few decades. However, a family in the congregation sponsored a Christian immigrant family from Myanmar/Burma. The man said, "I'm a Christian, others just say they are Christians. We are Christians." He was not bragging. This was his way of saying; with his limited English we take our faith seriously. Today those from Myanmar outnumber the Caucasians. How I rejoice in what God is doing.

Week Days

Mondays were "wash" days. We placed wet wash piece by piece between two rollers on the washing machine to remove much of the water before hanging it up in the backyard. In cold weather, it often froze before it was completely dry. Tuesday was ironing day. I don't remember a designation for Wednesday and Thursday, but Friday was cleaning day. Saturday was the day to prepare for Sunday dinner with potential guests. This meal was the finest meal of the week.

Occasionally on Saturday evening, Dad went to the store with a bowl, which he gave to the man behind the counter to fill with scoops of ice cream. What a treat! About every two weeks he went to the grocery store with a list, which he gave to the gentleman who filled the order from his shelves as we waited to pay the bill.

Grandmother Graver lived with us, although she died when I was 3 years old. I'm not sure I actually remember holding a rose to her nose as she lay in the casket, but I was told so often, it seems real to me. Today, to our detriment, I think we lose the reality of death by having the casket at the funeral home. Removing and denying the thought of death contributes to the frivolity of living.

Faith walked a few blocks up the street to a two-room school, with only one other girl in her class. Sometimes the teacher held Faith and the other girl on her lap as she taught. She usually received A's on her report card. Not so for me when I started first grade six years later, with more than 150 students in my elementary school.

One of my first memories was calling across the street to the neighbor boy. As I was talking with him, I shook the road sign in our front yard. A bumble bee came out of the metal sign post and stung me. That influenced my attitude toward bumble bees. Years later, I learned I was allergic to bee stings.

In 1942, when I was 5, my parents sold the property to a family in our church: house, barn and two or three acres for $3,000.

FARM LIFE

1942-1950

We moved to the David Shenk farm along New Danville Pike, about a mile or two west of Lancaster.[1] I enjoyed chasing my sister up and down the huge farm house's two stairways and all throughout its many rooms.

From our house's porch we could see the train tracks on the other side of the Conestoga River. I can still hear the train's shrill whistle. I often watched as the train sped up, anticipating the incline. If the train had too many cars, I knew what was going to happen: After the wheels began to spin, the engineer had to give up, back down the track, unhook a couple cars and try again.

Exciting But Dangerous

Farm life has many positives. When I was as young as 5 years old, Dad often invited me to drive the tractor, even though I was unable to reach the brake. He called or motioned from the wagon where he was stacking the hay as it came up the hay-loader to turn right or left so the loader would track the wind-row. When we came to the end of the row, he jumped off the wagon and grabbed the steering wheel to take me to the next wind-row. I loved this. It didn't take me long before I could make the turn, enabling the loader behind the wagon so it lined up with the next wind-row.

---

1 The grandson of David Shenk, David W. Shenk, is a resident here at Landis Homes. He is well known throughout the church having written 20 books and traveled the world influencing many thousands of Muslims to come to faith in Jesus Christ.

Dad also set me on his lap when he mowed hay. This upset Mother extremely. She knew that if I slipped from his knee and fell, I would have been cut severely or perhaps even killed.

By the time I was 10, I could back a four-wheeled wagon loaded with hay or straw bales into the barn within inches to the bale loader. During harvest we worked together with a neighbor farmer. One year, Dad would be away on church business when it was time to make hay, so a concerned neighbor asked, "Who will back the wagons for us?" Dad informed him that I would, and I felt proud.

We were taught never to be proud, so I should say, "I felt affirmed." I think one verse I heard from my mother more than any other was, "Pride goes before destruction, a haughty spirit before a fall." (Proverbs 16:18). A close second was, "Him that thinks he stands, take heed lest he falls." (I Corinthians 10:12 KJV).

Dad also took me along when he plowed the field bordering the Conestoga River. Dad got so close to the riverbank, I was fearful the dirt would give way and we would go tumbling the 4-plus feet into the river. By God's grace that never happened.

One day, we learned that our 8-year-old neighbor across the street in Conestoga had been electrocuted while mowing the lawn; he accidently ran over the electric lawn mower cord. I was asked to be one of his pallbearers. Mother was concerned that I was too young at age 7 to help carry the casket, yet with a heavy heart I did. His death made a deep impression on me.

Elementary School

This move to the farm affected my life more than any other period. Like most children I skipped kindergarten and started first grade in Lancaster City at age 5, which meant I was one of the youngest in my class. My farm life had also sheltered me from the rough urban life of many of my classmates with its unfamiliar standards, aggressive behavior and shocking language.

Each day, I walked 200 yards along the busy New Danville Pike to wait with LeRoy, a neighbor boy, for the daily, 30-minute bus ride. It seemed like a never-ending trip through parts of the poorer section of Lancaster City.

Occasionally during recess, students gathered in a big circle on the playground to watch two boys fight each other. I was frightened, seeing the blood mixed with tears and snot running from their faces. One of the faculty would look out the window, notice the situation and come hurriedly to put an end to the chaos.

Student patrol became one of the highlights of my elementary school experience. The captain of the patrol, with his broad shoulders, was the largest Black student in the school. Ruth, whom I found especially cute, and I were chosen as co-lieutenants. Wearing our shoulder belts and badges, we walked from block to block daily, ensuring that all other patrol guards were faithfully functioning at their assigned street crossings.

My grades hovered at average or a bit above. When I brought home C's, my mother merely said, "Hopefully it will be better next report period." Being a supersensitive child, I understood her to be disappointed in me. I felt I could not measure up to her expectations, no matter how hard I tried. I feel sure this contributed to my stuttering speech.

Stuttering – Major Problem

I don't remember exactly when I began to stutter, although I know I showed signs of this while we lived in Conestoga. Classmates frequently imitated my stuttering as the others laughed. Needless to say, this was painful and left deep scars that stayed with me for decades. I expect I will carry these vivid memories to my grave.

I remember hiding and crying at times, wishing I could die, although I was too embarrassed to admit this to anyone. I lived with fear that when someone asked me a question, I would have to stutter and be greatly embarrassed. One way I tried to compensate was to excel in sports. Here I received recognition even from those who laughed at my stuttering.

I thought someday I might conquer my speech impediment because I could speak to the cows fluently. I believed that if I could speak to the cows, I could learn to speak to people. Surprisingly, I could sing without stuttering. This gave me some hope in what I felt was a hopeless situation.

Looking back, I often wonder if my inferiority complex spawned my innate desire to lead. At the same time, perhaps my struggle to overcome that poor self-image served as a good exercise: learning to overcome the sins of the natural man that I was born with. Was God preparing me for a life of serving as a pastor? I believe God uses everything in our life, especially painful experiences, to help prepare and equip us for future service.

During the winter, Dad would prune the apple and peach trees in the large orchard. I helped gather those branches thick enough to burn in our kitchen stove. If Dad needed to remove an entire tree, he would split the logs, load them on a wagon and pile them near our wood shed. I helped him hold the logs for the large circular saw, which was run by a belt connected to the tractor pulley. Sawdust flew everywhere. This wood provided fuel for the kitchen stove in the winter.

In one of the large rooms of the house we placed an old kitchen table, then fastened a net across it. This provided many happy hours of pinpong for Faith and me.

World War II

WWII affected everyone. When the sirens blared at night, we had to turn off all lights in our house and barn. Gasoline was rationed, but farmers were permitted to purchase whatever gasoline they needed for their equipment, to cultivate and harvest the crops.

When air raid sirens sounded during school, teachers ushered us to the long hallway, where we knelt facing the wall until it was OK to return to our rooms. When our friend, Myrtle Nisley, talked with Mother on the phone describing her son's experiences in the war, you could hear the pain in her voice.

In 1945, I remember bringing the mail from the mailbox with the newspaper headline: "WWII Ends." What a relief!

When I was 6, we hosted the "Eshleman Family Reunion" in our barn. Imagine the work it took to provide a full meal for 75 persons. Dad made trusses and placed boards on them so we could all sit down together to eat. In the afternoon, the kids and a few adults played softball and other games while the adults enjoyed catching up on everyone's news.

Christmastime was special. Mother was an excellent cook. She made 5-gallon lard cans full of Christmas cookies. My favorite was her coconut cookies. For weeks, even into February, I would go to the cool basement archway after school and help myself to those cookies. Pie, usually apple, peach or cherry was found on the table throughout the year. Her cracker-pudding was a favorite of mine.

Corn Harvest

In the fall, we stored part of the corn crop in the silo for silage for the cows. Dad cut the remaining cornstalks at the base and formed them into corn shock. When the ears of corn dried, he husked them, tossed the corn on the wagon and shoveled it in the corn crib. After I got home from school, I often helped to see how many ears I could husk before milking time. Occasionally Jinks, our dog, chased out a mouse or rat, which he took care of in short order.

The eight-page *Youth Christian Companion* magazine came once a week. I would bring in the mail, and if farm work was not pressing after lunch, we sat around the kitchen table as Mother read the gripping story of Lucy Winchester by Christmas Carol Kauffman. We looked forward to hearing the next installment. I feel so blessed as I remember these times. Too often today we have allowed TV and iphones to rob us of time for family conversation.

A Clear Conscience

In the first grade when we returned from recess, Clarence was crying. The teacher asked if we knew what brought this about. When she called on me, I said I didn't know. My conscience bothered me for years after that. I finally wrote a letter to the teacher and the boy, asking for forgiveness for telling this lie.

Maybe I have a supersensitive conscience, but it was a relief to get my conscience cleared. Satan is "the accuser of the brethren." (Revelation 12:10, KJV). So whether we are age 6 or 86, guilt feelings will rob us of our joy and effectiveness for the Lord. Peter reminds us in 1 Timothy 1:19 that we are to hold onto a good conscience so we can be faithful witnesses.

At the annual Eshleman Christmas gathering, we pulled names to exchange gifts. For some reason when the gifts were handed out, I did not receive a gift. One of my uncles came to my rescue and gave me a gift. I believe God allowed that experience so I know what it feels like to be left out.

Chores

I had my usual chores after school. Around age 10, I climbed the silo to throw down silage for the cows and then helped distribute the silage in the cow trough. I didn't like climbing up or descending the wet silo ladder because it was slippery. I knew that if I lost my grip, I would fall many feet and be injured for life if not killed. Each Saturday I was expected to sweep clean the 120-foot by 12-foot forebay in front of our barn.

One summer during a storm, I received an electrical shock while walking barefoot on the cement forebay. I dreaded the frequent lightning and thunderstorms. We believed the storms often followed the Conestoga Creek just several hundred yards from the barn. Zechariah 10:1, "It is the Lord who sends the thunderstorms." Job asks, "Who can understand the thunder of His power?" (Job 26:14).

I believe it is good to live with a holy and reverent fear of God. Today, the overemphasis on God's love often ignores the fear of God, leaving us with a proud heart. "The fear of the Lord is the beginning of knowledge." (Proverbs 1:7).

When the cows didn't come to the barn at milking time, I called them. If they didn't respond to my call I went after them. I didn't mind walking in the meadow unless the bull was with them. I kept my eyes on that bull. I didn't trust him. I had nightmares of that bull chasing and crushing me. What a relief to wake up and find myself safely in bed. After years of this reoccurring dream, I prayed earnestly for God to remove it. Praise God, He did.

Did you know cows have a sweet tooth? Every two weeks, the hammer mill came to grind corn from our corncrib, as well as barley and wheat—all for cow feed. We'd add molasses to the mix so the cows would eat more and, we hoped, produce more milk. This molasses was stronger than the King Syrup sitting on our kitchen table beside the salt and pepper shaker. The cows would turn their heads following my every move until their turn came to have this corn chop put on their silage for supper.

A few times every summer I traveled with Dad on Mondays to the Lancaster Stockyards to take a calf to be sold to the butcher. Captivated, I watched how the buyers and sellers tracked the cattle through all the various pens that seemed to me like utter chaos.

Living Close to God's Nature

To grow crops, you need the right amount of rain. As Dad watched it rain, he would say, "That was a million-dollar present from God."

Dad often whistled hymns as he worked, ever conscious of God. How blessed I was to be in his presence. Not that he was perfect; at times he showed his anger, especially when the cows did not remember to go in their assigned stalls. At those times I learned to make myself scarce.

Farmers are always close to God's creation. When the corn was tall you could hear the approaching rains moving across the fields. If you were close to the barn, you could often run for shelter before the rain reached you. When you saw the lightning, you knew how far the lightning strike was from you by how long it took for the clap of thunder to reach your ears.

God gave us ears to hear Him and eyes to see Him if our minds are turned toward Him. It's a joy to live with a consciousness of God, who created all nature surrounding us. Theologian Martin Luther is often attributed as saying: "Our Lord has not written the promise of resurrection in books alone, but on every leaf of springtime."

Lesson From a Mule

We "inherited" a horse and mule when we moved to the farm. A mule is the offspring of a male donkey (jack) and a female horse (mare). Dad knew that our mule, Old Rose, would never make it to mule heaven. When given the call to turn right, Old Rose turned left and vice-versa. She was a good illustration for the apostle Paul's description of God's people as obstinate and disobedient (Romans 10:21). It didn't take long before Dad bought a small used tractor to replace the mule and horse team.

One Sunday afternoon our landlord's daughter, Ruth, led a group of young people on a hike to a cave along the ridge of the Conestoga Creek. The cave was only about 15 feet deep, but you could stand up in it. I found it fascinating, even mind-boggling, to think that some of the Susquehannock Indians might have lived there.

To keep the rainwater from eroding our dirt driveway, which led to the fields and orchard, my father had created breakers about a foot high every 75 feet. Once, while I was learning to ride my bicycle, I was going too fast and hit a breaker, messing up my bike and hurting myself. Rather than going to the house for some TLC and band-aids, I hid in the barn, embarrassed that I had fallen off my bike.

The world's largest flower clock was only a mile from our house. Occasionally, LeRoy and I would ride our bikes up the long hill on Hoover Road to Conestoga Memorial Park. When we stopped riding and stood still, we could actually observe the movement of the minute hand, likely 12 or 15 feet long. (The clock has long since been removed.) On our way home, while racing down that long hill on Hoover Road, we sounded the sirens mounted on our bikes to let the world know exactly where we were. The sirens were so shrill they are outlawed today.

As another unique feature of the park, upright tombstones were not permitted. Upkeep was easy, since you didn't have to trim around the tombstones. That so impressed me that, 75 years later, Helen and I chose a flat stone for our future memorial, which is in place at Habacker Mennonite Church south of Mountville, in Lancaster County.

Our landlord owned a 1927 Chevy pickup truck. When I was strong enough to lift a half bushel of apples or peaches, I loaded the truck in the orchard and drove it to the garage where the fruit was sorted. I loved to drive that old straight-shift truck. Imagine that the windshield wipers had to be powered by hand.

God's in the Dark

We tried to remember to close the chicken house doors to help keep the coons from getting in and killing the chickens. If we forgot to close the doors before dark, I had to go in the dark. It would have helped if I would have remembered God's promise in Psalm 139:12, and believed that the darkness will not be dark to us, the night will shine like the day, for the darkness is light to us.

My mother and Faith, usually gathered the eggs. Faith didn't like this job because the chickens picked your hand as you reached under them for the eggs. If they were too busy, I had to help gather the eggs. Mother helped with the morning and evening milking. When we got a milking machine, she made sure the milking equipment was washed clean.

To my knowledge, I was the only student at Burrows School that lived on a farm. When my third-grade teacher discovered this, she asked if I could bring her fresh eggs. I took my dad's large black metal lunch box and put in a dozen eggs along with my lunch. I delivered them to her whenever she wanted eggs.

This same teacher used to say, "Anyone who is not paying attention when I call on you to read will have a whack with this paddle." She only hit me once with her paddle. For me, that lasted for a lifetime.

A childhood joy I remember is when David Shenk, our landlord, took Faith and me to the Philadelphia Zoo and to the beach. Since Dad and Mother were raised during the Depression, they never considered taking us on a vacation. After all, the cows needed milked twice a day and the eggs needed to be gathered daily. All in all, Dad enjoyed his work. He taught me the joy of working. Unfortunately, I picked up his workaholic lifestyle. Life is more than work.

Church Life

We attended and participated in River Corner Mennonite Church. We were relieved that the lot for minister did not fall on Dad. For those not familiar, this method of choosing a minister was patterned from Acts 1:26 and other New Testament examples.

After seeking God's direction, the members would nominate people who were then examined, and if the bishops approved, they were entered into the lot. A slip of paper was placed in one Bible or hymnbook, and each candidate drew a book. The one with the paper was chosen. Tension was high to see who would be chosen as minister.

For several years, Dad served as Sunday school superintendent. Mother read the Bible each evening and made sure we said our prayers before we went to bed. We also offered silent prayer before each meal and usually followed the meal with a silent prayer of thanks.

I was not an especially good reader, but I think I read the Bible through by the time I was 10 or 12. Nearly always my mother made sure the Bible lay open on the kitchen table before we retired for bed. The idea was that if a thief or anyone tried to enter the house, they would have to walk past the open Bible. Many people in those days, even though they did not attend church, respected the Bible.

We must be careful not to use the Bible as a fetish. The Bible, unless inspired by the Holy Spirit, is simply another book. It has no power in itself. When the Holy Spirit is present the Bible is God's Word, inspired by God, it is "sharper than any double-edged sword, it penetrates even to dividing soul and spirit, it judges the thoughts and attitudes of the heart." (Hebrews 4:12). Many today use the cross as a fetish. Just hanging a cross around our neck or on earrings does not bring good luck. When the cross is preached proclaiming Jesus' death and resurrection it has the power to save for eternity. (I Corinthians 2:2).

I'll always remember the "Lord's Acre"—when a farmer would donate an acre of land for the youth from church to grow a crop. Tomatoes or potatoes were the usual choice. The youth helped in whatever way they could. We often spent evenings picking tomatoes and enjoying an ice cream snack after our hard work. All the proceeds went to our missionaries.

My Spiritual Birthday

Our Mennonite church was missionary minded, that is, they were concerned for anyone who did not know Jesus, so they started several churches in Lancaster City. One way to begin a church was to reach the community children, and Summer Bible School paved the way.

When I was 7, our landlord took Faith and me to Summer Bible School in Lancaster. On the last night of Bible school, the pastor told the account of Jesus dying for our sins and asked us to raise our hand if we wanted Jesus to come into our life. I raised my hand and cried as some of the others looked at me. I understood I needed forgiveness for my sins and Jesus could forgive me and give me eternal life. That was my spiritual birthday.

One aspect of Summer Bible School was to memorize Scripture. I remember memorizing Matthew 5. Over the years, Matthew 5 has been a definite bulwark to my faith. Even to this day, whenever I can't sleep, I recite much of Matthew 5 as well as Psalm 23. This works great. I have often preached on Jesus' eight steps into kingdom living, commonly called the Beatitudes (Matthew 5:3-12).

The Uncertainty of Life

During harvest time, my father sometimes helped another farmer from our church. When hay that is not dry or is too green is put into a barn, it can become hot and ignite. One day, neighboring farmers were in the field a distance from a barn when they saw the smoke billowing into the sky. I was in school, but that evening Dad took me with him to see the ruins.

I still remember the smell from burning flesh and the outline of the charred dairy cows in their stalls. At age 7, this made a deep impression on me concerning the brevity of life and how quickly earthly possessions can go up in smoke. Jesus said, "Don't store up treasures here on earth, where moths eat them and rust destroys them, and where thieves break in and steal. Store up your treasures in heaven." (Matthew 6:19-20, NLT).

A car stopped at our place and the driver asked to use the phone to call an ambulance. Another man in the car was gasping for breath. My dad and the driver helped the man to walk to our living room where he lay on the couch until the ambulance came. I thought the man was going to die.

In another incident my neighbor man died. The funeral with an open casket was in their living room. We sang the following song that speaks clearly to me even today:

This world is not my home, I'm just a passing through
My treasures are laid up somewhere beyond the blue;
The angels beckon me from heaven's open door,
And I can't feel at home in this world anymore.

O Lord, you know I have no friend like you,
If heaven's not my home, then Lord what will I do?
The angels beckon me from heaven's open door,
And I can't feel at home in this world anymore.

Mother had times of indigestion when she gasped for breath. As a child this frightened me; I feared she might die. Not long after these incidents, a teen at our church was killed in an auto accident. Death was real. Was I ready to die? Looking back now upon how those incidents elicited fear in me; I'm reminded how important it is to talk to children about life and death—and share about Jesus who offers eternal life (John 14:6).

Mottos and Mother's Musical Influence

My parents displayed several mottos and scriptural phrases on the wall of our home. One had a major influence on my life: "Your life will soon be past, only what's done for Christ will last."

I was always very time conscious, and I remember praying that I would live as long as Jesus lived, to age 33. Moses was also time conscious; he prayed that he would number his days so he'd be wise (Psalm 90:12). Realizing that life is short helps us use the little time we have more wisely and for eternal good. I learned to ask: What does God want me to accomplish in life and what step(s) can I take toward accomplishing that goal?

Another motto that affected me greatly was: "Say nothing you would not want to be saying when Jesus comes; do nothing you would not want to be doing when Jesus comes; and go nowhere you would not want to be when Jesus comes."

I like to turn this motto from negative to positive, so that it reads: "Say only what you would want to be saying when Jesus comes. …" Jesus reminds us that we, like those in Noah's time, will be caught unaware of His coming (Matthew 24:36-42).

If we remain mindful of Jesus' eventual return, this can help keep our focus on His eternal presence and His watchful and loving eye. "I will counsel you with my loving eye on you." (Psalm 32:8). And, "The eyes of the Lord are everywhere, keeping watch on the wicked and the good." (Proverbs 15:3).

Mother frequently played the piano after supper, when Faith and I joined her in singing the great hymns of the church. Mother often expressed her desire for me to be a music conductor. This never materialized, as I could sing the melody but was never proficient at singing baritone, which was more in my voice range. Music is God's universal and eternal language.

How blessed I was to have a mother to teach me these hymns. They reverberate through my mind even today.

The large farm also gave me plenty of space to be alone with

God. Often, as I walked the back dirt road leading to the farm fields and the orchard, I talked with Him—my little mind trying to comprehend His purpose for my life. If Jesus got alone with His Father, how much more do we need to get alone with God? (Mark 1:35). Parents, model talking to God as you walk in His creation. Let your children hear you talking to God as you would talk to your friend.

Fall From the Swing

Once a year we attended the "Graver Family Reunion" at Long's Park in Lancaster, where my older cousin took me on the swing with him. He kept pumping, going higher and higher until the chains were not taunt, causing the swing to jerk as it fell free for several feet. I fell hitting the hard ground, where I was knocked unconscious. I remember waking up, surrounded by people looking at me.

Frequently, people walking along the highway stopped at our house asking for food. They were without a job or home, and others referred to them as tramps. Mother prepared a good hot meal for them which they ate on our porch. One man slept on a bed of straw in our cow stable. I could smell when he was there because he drank canned heat—mostly alcohol—which he strained through his sock.

About this time, I had to have my tonsils and adenoids removed. Before then, I had never been away from home overnight. I also had never visited a hospital, and I didn't like its smell. I remember seeing the nurses lined up on both sides of my bed. They held me down until I inhaled enough ether to put me out. Thank God they have much simpler ways of putting children to sleep today.

Revival Meetings and Baptism

The River Corner Church held two weeks of revival meetings in the spring and fall each year. I enjoyed these times, because the guest ministers were easy to listen to, with their accounts of God's leading often in dramatic or unusual ways.

Frequently, these evangelists introduced us to a new chorus. One that meant a lot to me was, "The Cleansing Wave," by Joseph Knapp.

Oh, now I see the crimson wave!

The fountain deep and wide;
Jesus, my Lord, mighty to save,
Points to His wounded side.

Refrain: The cleansing stream I see, I see!
I plunge, and, oh, it cleanseth me!
Oh, praise the Lord, it cleanseth me!
It cleanseth me, yes, cleanseth me.

I rise to walk in Heav'n's own light,
Above the world and sin,
With heart made pure and garments white,
And Christ enthroned within.

Amazing grace! 'tis Heav'n below
To feel the blood applied,
And Jesus, only Jesus know,
My Jesus crucified.

By age 10, when we had revival meetings, I stood when the invitation was given and expressed a desire to be baptized, but my parents thought it would be best if I understood more before I made this commitment of a lifetime. The following year they were convinced I was serious and readily gave their consent.

Jesus said, "He who believes – [that is,] who adheres to and trusts in and relies on the Gospel and Him Whom it sets forth – and is baptized will be saved [from the penalty of eternal death]; but he who does not believe – who does not adhere to and trust in and rely on the Gospel and Him Whom it sets forth – will be condemned." (Mark 16:16 AMP).

In the catechism class before baptism, we focused on Jesus' Sermon on the Mount, Matthew 5-7. These chapters are often highlighted when people ask, "What do Mennonite's believe?"

At baptism, we confessed before the congregation that Jesus Christ is Lord. We confessed our sinful nature and asked Jesus to forgive us and enable His Holy Spirit to help us live faithfully for Christ until death. We also promised to be faithful to our church by being willing to both receive and give counsel to one another.

The Mennonite Church is in the Anabaptist stream of theology. Anabaptism is not anti-Baptist. *Ana* means "another"; therefore anabaptism means another baptism besides infant baptism. Our belief is that infants do not have the ability to make a life-time commitment because of their lack of understanding. We believe parents cannot do this for their children.

Instead, Mennonites practice believer's baptism, which means that once a person is old enough to understand their need for a Savior, they must confess their sins and commit themselves to Jesus Christ for life—the most important decision of our life.

While we do not baptize babies, we provide a dedication service for parents to dedicate their children to God. In this simple service, the parents promise to do all they can to raise their children to follow Jesus. The congregation also pledges their support.

JUNIOR HIGH AND HIGH SCHOOL

1947-1954

Junior high school, on President Avenue in Lancaster, offered more challenges with its larger enrollment. We moved from room to room for our various classes. I easily felt lost.

At noon, many students left to visit the local candy store, spending what, to me, was lots of money on the pinball machines, along with ice cream and candy. Our family was not poor but we were frugal, so this kind of spending felt totally foreign. I admit I was a bit envious; I would have loved to have a nickel for the pinball machine so I could prove I'd win.

Nevertheless, my parents were not frugal when it came to giving in the church and to helping relatives in need, including strangers, with produce from our large garden.

My parents demonstrated that "God loves a cheerful giver." (II Corinthians 9:7). What they taught me and modeled for me about the saving of money and giving to others in need has blessed me throughout my life. "The generous will be blessed." (Proverbs 22:9).

Learning and Growing

When taking a standardized test at school, I walked past another student's desk and saw an answer I did not know. While I tried to rationalize that I would have guessed the same answer he had, I felt guilty. Ashamed, I apologized.

Field Day provided an opportunity to show our skills. I'd try as hard as I could to get a little recognition by winning in these events, even practicing at home. I remember cherishing a couple of ribbons I received on Field Day.

Often, the neighbor boys who lived close to Lancaster came with their basketball to play in our barn. My dad kept the farm equipment crowded into other places just so that we could have space for basketball, where we soon wore the floorboards smooth with our running up and down the court. We also built tunnels with straw bales and jumped off the rafters into the loose hay in the mow. In the winter we went sledding.

I loved harvest time. My cousin, Chet Eshleman, brought his combine to harvest our barley and wheat crops. I was amazed to see how fast the bags of grain filled. Mother would bring lemonade for the hot, thirsty men in the fields.

I admired my cousin's new 1950 Ford. He took me for a ride. What a thrill to go 50 miles an hour! One time he brought Grandpa Eli Eshleman with him—the only time I remember meeting my grandpa. Despite being rather frail, Grandpa impressed me with his glass eye. He died soon after that visit, at age 80. I missed a lot, not having a relationship with any of my grandparents.

Central Manor

When I was 13, my parents bought a farm at Central Manor, between Millersville and Washington Borough in Lancaster County. This meant I had to change schools to complete the last couple months of my eighth grade.

This smaller rural school atmosphere was very congenial. I felt the eighth-grade teacher took a special liking to me, perhaps sympathizing with how I had to change schools with only a few weeks away from eighth-grade "graduation." She called attention to how polite I was, which was embarrassing as well as affirming.

Habacker Mennonite Church

For the first year after we moved, we continued to drive in our 1933 DeSoto each Sunday to River Corner Church. But since my mother had a few distant relatives at Habacker Mennonite Church, only 3 miles from our farm, we started attending and soon became active members. When I was old enough to drive, I participated in the Wednesday evening prayer meeting with the pastors and several others. I was the only one anywhere close to my age.

Habacker Mennonite Church was built on a plot of land purchased in 1724 from Thomas and Richard Penn, sons of William Penn. The original deed states that the land was to be used by the Anabaptists for a place of worship, a school and a burial ground. My future mother-in-law's maiden name was Habacker. The school she attended is no longer there, but the church building and cemetery are still in use. In fact, my wife, Helen (Steffy), and I plan to be buried there beside her parents and several other relatives.

At the time we started attending, the Habacker congregation was in decline. Years later, things started to turn around when one of the families hosted an immigrant family from Myanmar (Burma). The loving care of the members drew more Karan People from Burma who lived in Lancaster; now, they outnumber the Caucasian members. Attendance is averaging 120.

These Burmese people are from a different area in Myanmar than those participating in River Corner Mennonite Church mentioned earlier. When different nationalities worship together, it's a glimpse of heaven. Helen and I rejoice that the church is growing again.

High School and My Growing Faith

During my high school years, the Youth for Christ organization impacted my life. Every Saturday night at Lancaster's YMCA, a hundred or more youth gathered for an enthusiastic and powerful presentation of the Gospel, sometimes using Billy Graham films. On different occasions I rededicated my life to Christ during the altar call following those films.

Often zeal is not related to Christian faith. Wayne would come home from work, grab his model airplane equipment and head for the grass field behind his house. The neighbor children soon heard the roar of his tiny but loud model airplane engines and came running to watch the stunts.

When Wayne's wife brought him his supper, he barely took time to eat. He was focused. He spent money, time and long hours of painstaking effort building planes, which frequently crashed into the ground after a few seconds in flight. His zeal for his hobby became his life.

I think: What would happen if our zeal for Jesus would move to that level? As Proverbs 23:17 tells us, "Always be zealous for the fear of the Lord." Paul admonishes us, "Whatever you do, work at it with all your heart, as working for the Lord." (Colossians 3:23).

On rainy days, with schoolwork completed, I enjoyed working with a jigsaw. I cut dozens of boards to use as whatnot shelves and gave them to mother's friends. Since most women sewed, I made spool holders by cutting out a board in the shape of a rooster. I placed the rooster on a base, to hold 10 different color spools of thread and painted them. Many of mother's friends bought them for a dollar.

We contracted with Consumers Packing Company to plant 4 acres of baby lima beans. After they were up and growing the biplane or double winged plane would spray the field. It was breathtaking to watch the plane swoop down a couple feet from the ground and then at the end of the rows suddenly lift up at a 45-degree angle just missing the telephone and electric wires hanging between their poles.

Leading Songs

When I was ages 9-11, my mother had persuaded me to take piano lessons. I did not excel, but I did learn the basics. Music was an important aspect of our worship services at Habacker Church. Ivan Charles, the song leader, showed an interest in me during my later years of high school; he taught me how to use the pitchpipe and instructed me on the fundamentals of leading and directing church music. By age 15, I led our congregational hymns.

I spent endless times practicing using my pitchpipe and beating time, often in the cow stable in preparation for Sunday worship. Since I stuttered, one of my challenges was announcing hymn numbers. I never stuttered on the word "eight" so I liked to choose the "eight" numbers.

Today, 70 years later, those hymns and Gospel songs still reverberate through my mind 24/7. Nearly every morning, I thank God for waking me with these praise hymns. I see this as an expression of Paul's admonition from prison in Ephesians 5:18-20, "Be filled with the Spirit, speaking to one another with psalms, hymns, and songs from the Spirit. Sing and make music from your heart to the Lord, always giving thanks to God the Father for everything, in the name of our Lord Jesus Christ."

The Christian Workers Band, the name of our Habacker Church youth group, often joined the youth from Mountville and Masonville

Churches for various activities. (Masonville is now Living Light Mennonite Church.) Sometimes we delivered *The Way,* which was similar to a Gospel tract. We drove to Washington Borough and covered the town, knocking on doors, encouraging people with this four-page paper. I'm sure we would have seen more fruit if we would have deliberately taken time to dialogue with the people.

A mile from our home, the Church of God owned Central Manor Campground. Each summer, for nine days—from Saturday through the following Sunday—hundreds of people stayed in the two-room cabins scattered throughout the campground. People spend their vacation there, enjoying Christian fellowship and listening to Gospel messages. I benefited from the powerful preaching of evangelist John R. Rice. On the final Sunday night hundreds of people marched around the large tabernacle, joyfully singing, "We're Marching to Zion."

I was excited when Dad purchased a '47 Chevy two-door coupe. This two-toned tan car came with several accessories, including a radio, which we didn't have in our home. On Sunday mornings I went out before church to listen to the Old Fashion Revival Hour with Charles E. Fuller. The powerful music and vigorous preaching thrilled my heart as a teen. I also enjoyed the Phillies' games on the car radio.

Tent Revival with George R. Brunk

One year in particular, East Chestnut Street Mennonite Church in Lancaster prayed and fasted for revival. They'd invited George R. Brunk from Harrisonburg, Virginia, to hold a tent revival. Nearly 2,000 people came the first night. The revival continued seven weeks, with an estimated 15,000 people attending on the final night. I was thrilled to see hundreds walk the sawdust trail to accept Christ or rededicate their life. Another result of the revival: Some farmers were convicted of the evils of tobacco and destroyed the tobacco plants in their fields.

I also enjoyed the annual Atglen hymning in Chester County. For this event, thousands, both young and old, gathered in this cow pasture/woods to sing and socialize all afternoon.

Bob, my best friend, took me to Youth for Christ meetings. I remember when his father died suddenly from a heart attack. The week after the funeral on Sunday afternoon, I went to see him, and over the years Bob repeatedly thanked me for that visit. From that experience, I learned the importance of visitation and the value of encouragement. It wasn't so much what I said, it was my presence that counted. On other Sunday afternoons, Bob and I and others might gather at Henry Bowman's farm to play softball in the summer or basketball in their barn in winter.

After church on Sunday evening my friend and I occasionally visited an African American church in Lancaster. In the 1950s it was inappropriate to call an African American church a Black church. We found their style of worship invigorating. Our Mennonite Church could use a little more of the enthusiasm and joy they expressed in their worship.

Speaking Out About Jesus

Throughout my four years at Penn Manor High School, I walked a half mile to the Central Manor Store to get on the school bus. Occasionally, a gentleman slowly puffing on his cigar while driving a huge tractor trailer would stop to pick me up. I will long remember his kindness, which was especially welcomed when it was near zero and blowing snow. Even more importantly, he helped me lay aside my fears and prejudice, as his skin color was different than mine.

Each day, high school opened with a salute to our nation's flag, followed by 10 verses of Scripture read by a student, then the reciting of the Lord's Prayer. I took my turn, reading and leading even though my stuttering made this experience difficult. Our school seldom scheduled Wednesday after-school activities because everyone reserved Wednesday evening as church night.

I participated in a weekly Bible Club, where we challenged each other to place the Bible on top of our other books as we went throughout the school day, in hopes this would be a positive testimony. "God's word is truth." (John 17:17). The Apostle Paul reminds us that God's Word is also profitable for instruction and training in righteousness or right living (II Timothy 3:16-17). Today many schools do not permit a Bible to be quoted or seen in the classroom.

Our senior class traveled by bus to Washington, D.C., for our class outing. While there, a street vendor encouraged people to record themselves for 25 cents, after which he would give them the flimsy disk to play on their victrola at home.

I had dreamed of being a radio preacher like Billy Graham, so this was intriguing and inviting to me. Because I stuttered, though, I was too intimidated to "preach" in front of this small crowd, so I asked my buddy, Johnny Frey if he would sing with me, "Just a Little Talk With Jesus."

Youth for Christ quartets had made this song popular among church people. So on a main street in D.C. close to the capitol we sang Reverend Cleavant Derrick's hymn:

I once was lost in sin, but Jesus took me in
And then a little light from heaven filled my soul.
He bathed my heart in love, and He wrote my name above
And just a little talk with Jesus makes me whole.

Refrain: Now let us have a little talk with Jesus,
Let us tell Him all about our troubles
He will hear our faintest cry. He will answer by and by.
When you feel a little prayer wheel turning
And you will know a little fire is burning
You will find a little talk with Jesus makes it right. (all right).

I may have doubts and fears, my eye be filled with tears
But Jesus is a friend who watches day and night.
I go to him in prayer, he knows my every care
And just a little talk with Jesus makes it right.

Agricultural Projects

Muskrats were a problem in my neighbor John Harnish's cow pasture. Since I was looking for ways to earn some money, I talked to Dad about trapping muskrats. I didn't know how to skin muskrats, however, and wasn't excited about learning. It was a relief when Dad said he'd skin them for me.

On frigid winter mornings it was difficult to get out of a warm bed to check my traps before school. Each evening, I checked my traps again to be sure they were set before dark. I soon found out it was not a money-making proposition.

Being in the agricultural curriculum track in high school I needed a farm project. Dad provided space in the barn for me to raise 300 broilers two or three times a year. We purchased day-old chicks and raised them for about 12 weeks until they weighed 3-4 pounds. A family who had a stand at the Lancaster Market purchased, dressed and sold the broilers for me. This project provided much of my needed funds toward college expenses.

In addition to raising broilers, I purchased a sow to raise piglets. This enhanced my possibility of receiving the Keystone State Farmer Degree, awarded by the Future Farmers of America. The piglets did well. Imagine my delight when I received this hard-earned degree.

The ag students went to the York County Fair. I admit I remember more clearly the motorcycles going around and around the 25-foot diameter silo than I remember the agriculture displays. These guys chased each other up and down the walls of the silo as they went round and round about 50 miles an hour—my estimate.

I would have loved to play on the school basketball team, but that was not possible. Dad had to milk and tend the cows, so he couldn't drive to Millersville and pick me up after practice. Midway into the season, with the junior varsity team floundering, the coach invited me to join them. His invitation meant so much, even though I couldn't accept.

During the summer, though, I joined a local softball league and was delighted that they asked me to be pitcher. I learned to swim on hot summer days when neighbor boys drove me to a local farm pond. In the dead of winter, those farm ponds froze over sufficiently, so we could ice skate. Frequently, we built a fire to roast marshmallows—a great way to meet and chat with the girls.

Heart Problem

In my junior year, at age 15, I developed a heart condition and missed five months of school. The doctor referred to my condition as an open valve of the heart. While they didn't call it rheumatic fever, I believe this is what it was. Doctors ordered plenty of rest.

One night during my convalescence I woke to Christmas caroling from our church youth group. I thought I must be in heaven. What a precious memory.

Thankfully, the school provided a tutor, who came every two weeks to assist me. During this time, I enjoyed reading books about missionaries and other inspirational books. I remember reading Charles Sheldon's *In His Steps*, Mrs. Howard Taylor's *Borden of Yale* and Roy Hession's *The Calvary Road*. These books made a powerful impact on me, especially *The Calvary Road,* which helped explain the work of the Holy Spirit and the need for brokenness. I'm sure this time further enhanced my desire to be a pastor. Looking back, I thank God for my "heart condition," which helped to change my life.

COLLEGE YEARS

1954-1958

I felt a call to be a pastor. There were no blinding lights from heaven but a definite conviction that this is what I need to do with my life. This sense of God's call is important. If you sense a person loves the Lord encourage them to dedicate their life to serving the Lord whether in the church or in a secular job. Surveys indicate that more than half the pastors in the U.S. would leave their job if they could find another position. Without a sense of call there is little or no passion, it's just a job. Paul preached, "not simply with words but with power, with the Holy Spirit and deep conviction." (I Thessalonians 1:5). He tells Timothy that the Holy Spirit God gives us is a Spirit of power, love and self-discipline (II Timothy 1:7). "God's Word is in my heart like a fire, a fire shut up in my bones. I am weary of holding it in; indeed, I cannot." (Jeremiah 20:9).

It took courage to go to the principal's office in December of my senior year. I told him, "I have decided to go to college; perhaps I better change a couple of classes so I'm more prepared for my freshman year." He placed me in the first-year algebra class.

In September after graduation, I entered Millersville State Teacher's college (now Millersville University), located across the street from our high school. I was in the freshman college algebra class, where most students were men attending under the GI Bill. No one else in the class had taken only one year of high school algebra. I prayed and studied long hours to understand the material. By God's grace I passed.

My tuition for that first year totaled $120. My books cost more than my tuition. No matter what class I took—biology, general science or world geography—I was confronted with the theory that we arrived where we are through the process of atheistic evolution. This challenged my belief and tested my faith that God was my creator. With prayer and a few Christian colleagues, I not only kept the faith but grew in my conviction of God as my creator.

Summer Jobs

Shortly after we moved to Central Manor, we met John Harnish, a neighbor dairy farmer. He asked if I could mow their lawn. For the next few years, I worked on his farm during my summers. I also painted his barn, killed turkeys and operated his hay baler on my college breaks—baling more than 10,000 hay and straw bales one summer. This along with helping other farmers on occasion helped provide the necessary funds toward my college education.

More important than earning money, however, I enjoyed the many discussions I had with John about church and the Christian life. I wrote a Gospel tract titled "One Thousand Years from Now," although I never published it. I like to think I was like David in the Bible, who said that his soul followed hard after God (Psalm 63:8, KJV).

Nearly 50 years later, I visited John Harnish in hospice. He told me how he remembered hearing me sing Gospel songs on the tractor as I was plowing, cultivating corn or raking hay. This brought back memories of singing "My God and I Go in the Field Together":

My God and I go in the field together;
We walk and talk as good friends should and do;
We clasp our hands, our voices ring with laughter;
My God and I walk through the meadow's hue.

He tells me of the years that went before me
When heavenly plans were made for me to be;
When all was but a dream of dim reflection;
To come to life, earth's verdant glory see.

My God and I will go for aye together,
We'll walk and talk just as good friends do;
This earth will pass, and with it common trifles,
But God and I will go unendingly.

I enjoyed helping my dad do the spring plowing with our two-bottom plow, which we pulled with our Allis-Chalmers tractor. The plow hitch was designed to trip when the plow hit a rock. Often rocks lay hidden under the top soil so you couldn't anticipate them. When I was going up an incline, I hit a rock that unhitched the plow. When I pushed in the clutch the tractor drifted back into the plow, causing one of the iron levers used to adjust the depth of the plow to slide off my back and between the spokes of the steering wheel.

I was sure God spared my life, because I could have been seriously injured. There were other times, especially when operating the baler, that I was also aware of God's protection. The consciousness of that protection helped me recognize that God had a plan for my life.

Today when you see a plowed field remember Hosea's words from the Lord, "Plow up the hard ground of your hearts, for now is the time to seek the Lord, that he may come and shower righteousness upon you. Plant the good seeds of righteousness, and you will harvest a crop of my love." (Hosea 10:12 NLT).

I now wish the Allis-Chalmers had a muffler, as it was extremely noisy and did damage to my hearing that I suffer from today. Yet I must admit: I loved to hear it backfire as the noise echoed through the valley.

That summer I led the singing for the more than 100 children at Mountville Mennonite Church Summer Bible School. Their enthusiasm encouraged everyone. I believe those choruses will remain with them for life. The following summer I taught the adult class. I thank God for their patience allowing me this privilege.

Discerning God's Call

Our pastors encouraged the men to wear a "plain" coat in contrast to a lapel. Since I believed that God wanted me to be a pastor, I felt I had better cooperate. Plain coats were definitely not popular with youth my age. I seldom wore the plain coat except when I went to Habacker Church.

Because of our ultraconservative bishop, most young men left our church. The good news is that they became active members in other churches. Their strong disciplined home life and the good solid biblical teaching at home and church kept them in the faith. I was tempted to leave as well, but I felt God wanted me to stay.

I struggled with the call of being a pastor. Like Moses, I stuttered, so I told myself, *I can't preach.* Also, I loved to operate farm machinery. Pastors in the Mennonite Church usually earned their own living, and I knew it was difficult to be a farmer and a preacher at the same time. I told the Lord: I am willing to give up farming if I can sell farm machinery. Clearly, I was struggling to discern God's leading.

Eastern Mennonite College

After my first year of college, I matriculated as a sophomore to Eastern Mennonite College, now Eastern Mennonite University, in Harrisonburg, Virginia. This move was painful for Mother. I'm sure she expected me to continue with the farm as she told Helen different times over the years that we would live in part of the house. Leaving her overprotective care was necessary for my healthy development. To ease her disappointment, I assured her I would write each week.

Each morning we were required to attend chapel, where college students sat together with students from the high school located just off the college campus. I ended up sitting side-by-side with *another* David Eshleman—the son of Dr. Merle Eshleman, missionary for many years to Tanganyika, Africa.

The congregation acapella music was inspiring. The college held "spiritual life week" each spring and fall, when the daily chapel services were lengthened. I remember attending frequent prayer sessions in the attic of the administration building. Students were called upon to open most every class with a prayer.

Foreign Languages – Not My First Love

As a Bible major, I took the required Spanish and Greek classes. I spent many nights trying to comprehend and memorize the foreign words. The first summer after taking Spanish, I used my limited vocabulary to communicate with the workers from Puerto Rico who came to the neighboring farm to pick tomatoes. However, after struggling with these languages, I decided the Lord was not calling me to be a missionary, even though I always greatly appreciated hearing missionary speakers.

Hebrew was also required during my senior year and into my first two years of seminary. Throughout my lifetime of pastoring, I was most thankful for studying Greek, mainly to check on word meaning and verb tenses. Yet I have become rusty with both Greek and Hebrew, since I am not preaching regularly.

Many evenings I walked to the top of the hill behind the administration building, where my dormitory was located. There I sat, overlooking the city of Harrisonburg with the Massanutten Mountain jutting into the sky, pointing to God. I spent time talking with Jesus, interceding for the lost people of the world and for Christians to be faithful. Paul commanded us to pray for all Christians everywhere (Ephesians 6:18). To me, Jesus is more intimate than God since Jesus walked this earth in flesh and blood like mine. Most Christians find it easier to talk about God than to talk about Jesus. The devil does not want you to mention Jesus. "No one can say, Jesus is Lord, except by the Holy Spirit." (I Corinthians 12:3).

During my junior year, my roommate Eugene Hostetter, invited me to Ridgeway Mennonite Church in Harrisburg. He urged me to drive the church bus. I took my role seriously: knocking on doors and urging the people to come. Joking, I would say, "I'll have to get you out of bed and dress you if you don't come."

Forty-nine years later, Eugene died of cancer. I went to his funeral and met Samuel Smucker, Ridgeway's pastor while we were in school. This was the first time I had seen him since those student years. He met me with the words, "You're the persistent bus driver."

The Smithsonian's Club on campus offered some diversion from my studies—with its socials and participation on the basketball and softball teams. It also was an excellent way to entertain my date. Eugene was part-time athletic director. Different times he had me oversee physical education classes, which I enjoyed.

For two years, I was honored to have Indiga Asfaw, a student from Ethiopia, as my roommate. Indiga had come to the United States through contacts made by Eastern Mennonite Missions, our mission board.

Indiga taught me some valuable lessons. One time I apparently forgot some of my clothes, which I left behind in Pennsylvania. He insisted I use some of his clothes, even though he had very little to share. More importantly, he taught me how to pray. He would kneel down to pray and stay on his knees for extended periods of time. He was a blessing to the whole school. Today, Indiga is one of the leading brain surgeons in our nation.

Love at First Sight?

Each summer during college, I returned to worship at Habacker Church. Between Sunday school and the worship service, the congregation listened as someone presented a children's story. This particular Sunday, Helen Steffy, impressed me with how she presented the Bible story and interacted with the children. I said to myself, *I'm going to learn to know that girl.*

I went to her house and asked if I could have a date to take her to church, but she had promised to babysit for her aunt. I thanked her and left. Her Grandmother Habacker told her, "He will be back."

The following summer after graduating from college, Helen also graduated from Lancaster Mennonite High School, and I again asked her for a date. This time things worked out. I planned to lead the singing Sunday evening at Wintertown Mennonite Church in York County, about 30 miles away, and she agreed to go with me—as well as a few of her friends who needed transportation.

Thereafter, our dates consisted of going to church, frequently with another young couple, then coming back to the house to play games and enjoy snacks. Helen nearly always had Gospel music playing in the background. The song "Others," by Charles Meigs, has served as a guiding principle for our lives:

Lord, let me live from day to day,
In such a self-forgetful way,
That even when I kneel to pray,
My pray'r shall be for others.

Refrain: Yes, others, Lord, yes, others,
Let this my motto be;
Help me to live for others,
Help me to live for others,

That I may live like Thee,
That I may live like Thee.

Help me in all my work I do
To ever be sincere and true,
And know that all I'd do for you
Must needs be done for others.

This theme of living for others has been our lifetime goal and lifestyle. We ended nearly every date by praying together. Prayer not only drew us closer to God, it drew us closer to each other.

I think it was on our first date that I learned Helen had read three books that week. I was impressed. Incidentally, in most of the 62 years since then, Helen has read dozens of books each year. One year she surpassed 200. She reads to assist pain control. After graduating from Lancaster Mennonite School, Helen began work at Lancaster General Hospital in its Central Supply Department.

I was asked to be a director at Black Rock Camp, a few miles southeast of Quarryville, in Lancaster County. What a wonderful opportunity—keeping 40 or more energetic youth challenged to walk with Christ. The key: dedicated cabin counselors and a camp pastor who could hold their interest in morning and evening chapel. Many young people made lifetime decisions to follow Jesus.

SEMINARY AND STUDENT PASTOR

1958-1961

Before I left for my first year of seminary, Helen and I agreed to continue our relationship via snail mail. Needless to say, I looked forward to her letters. Phone calls were not even considered, because of the expense. In my six years at school in Virginia, I don't think I made more than two or three long-distance calls. Of course, during school breaks we took every opportunity to grow our relationship.

Seminary students were required to have field experience. I was assigned to a student pastorate with Dr. J. Otis Yoder as my field advisor. This meant traveling about 20 miles each Sunday to Mt. Jackson Mennonite Church. The church, originally started by EMC students, met in a building that had been used during the Civil War as a hospital for soldiers.

At 8:30 a.m. each Sunday, I drove EMC's VW bus with six college students—each of us carrying packed lunches for our noon and evening meals. I often picked up people for either Sunday school or worship. We helped with Sunday school, and I alternated with Dr. Yoder to preach every other Sunday.

In the afternoons, we visited church members and people in the community. For the evening service, Dr. Yoder and the leadership team assigned a topic to college students or persons from the community. After a long day, we said goodbye and boarded the VW bus—arriving back on campus about 9 p.m.

One time, Dr. Yoder told me he had to speak at a conference and would be out of town most of the week. He had learned that a man living in the mountains near Mt. Jackson was on the verge of dying. I should be prepared to handle the funeral service—meeting the people and delivering the message. This was a new experience for me. I spoke on "Thy Will be Done"—the first of more than 125 funerals in my pastoral ministry of 50+ years.

While my Sunday experiences greatly shaped me and my future ministry, my seminary years gave me so many other memorable moments. I remember when Dr. C. K. Lehman pointed out Ephesians 2:6: "God raised us up with Christ and seated us with Him in the heavenly realms in Christ Jesus." That verse has stuck with me these past 60 years. If I really believe that verse, there is no room for worry, discouragement or depression. How wonderful are the promises of God!

Painting

The following summer I worked on a paint crew with men who knew more about the world than I cared to know or wanted to know. Paul said that he was crucified to the world and the world was crucified to him. (Galatians 6:14). The first week I was assigned to painting window sashes with six individual panes. What a tedious job. I didn't enjoy climbing to the top of the 40-foot extension ladder, but it was a way to earn money for my tuition. A more enjoyable experience was painting my future in-laws' house.

In my spare time I painted the gable end of our barn. Our 36-foot extension ladder was not long enough to reach the peak so dad helped me by placing a wagon with hay bales beside the barn. We then placed the ladder on top of the bales to reach the peak. Not the safest arrangement! I'm glad painting is not my vocation.

Engagement and Wedding

I persuaded Helen to enroll in EMC. Even though I was a second-year seminary student and student pastor, because of Helen's age, we needed a chaperone to accompany us on a date unless it was a campus function. We accepted these restrictions without much thought because we seldom went off campus. We looked forward to spending every Sunday together at Mt. Jackson.

One day in the fall of my second year of seminary, I asked Helen to take a two-hour hike with me to the top of Massanutten. Our chaperone lingered behind on purpose. We sat there overlooking the endless valley of farmland before I asked the question. On her promise to marry me, we shared our first kiss. I jokingly said, "You had to consent or I would have jumped off the cliff." When we went home for Easter break, I asked Helen's parents, Chester and Elizabeth Steffy, if I could marry their daughter. They agreed!

It was customary when announcing an engagement for marriage to post the announcement on the school bulletin board and leave campus. After posting our engagement picture and announcement, we drove south on Route 11 to Natural Bridge, Virginia. It was a cloudy, rainy day. Near the end of our tour the sun dramatically broke through the clouds, producing a brilliant rainbow over the bridge. We were sure God had placed it just for us—a clear indication of His blessing upon our lives.

We were married at Habacker Mennonite Church on August 13, 1960. Helen was 19 and I was 23. Beforehand, we had to meet with our very conservative bishop to be sure we were following his dress code. I had my plain suit, which pleased him. Helen agreed to wear a cape dress, which is an extra layer of material that covers from the shoulders to the waist for modesty reasons. She wore black shoes for the wedding but asked him for permission to put white shoes in the back of the church to wear for the wedding pictures. The bishop gave his permission. We wanted to respect him and follow Paul's advice to "live in harmony with one another." (Romans 12:16).

Herbert Schultz, my Canadian roommate in seminary, gave the wedding message. The congregation sang, "O Perfect Love" as the bridal party entered and Helen walked down the aisle. Everyone joined in singing a hymn Helen and I both cherished, "Joyful, Joyful, We Adore Thee."

We celebrated our wedding meal with over 100 guests in Hostetter's Dining Hall in Mt. Joy, (now called The Gathering Place), while the EMC men's quartet graced the atmosphere with their harmonious acapella music. That evening, we left for our honeymoon to the New England States in our '57 Chevy decorated with streamers. We looked forward to hiking in the White Mountains of New Hampshire and riding the ski lift, viewing the mountains and waterfalls.

Honeymoon

The first night of the honeymoon, I accidentally locked my keys in the car, which we didn't discover until the next morning.

Fortunately, someone who had the skills to unlock the car came to our rescue.

While traveling through Boston, we visited Old North Church, Boston's oldest Episcopal surviving church building, built in 1723. On the eve of April 18, 1775, two men had climbed the steeple and held high two lanterns as a signal from Paul Revere that the British were marching to Lexington and Concord. This fateful event ignited the American Revolution.

Before our wedding, Eastern Mennonite Mission had asked us to consider leading a youth cell group that they wanted to launch in Portland, Maine. We had declined EMM's offer, because I felt called to pastoral work. However, while we were in the area, we visited Portland and ended up taking a swim in the Atlantic Ocean. We believed that sunburn would be no problem that far north. We learned fast.

Driving south, we stopped in New York City to visit some friends. All in all, we enjoyed traveling through one state to the next on our way, as well as getting to know each other more intimately.

Before heading back to seminary, we promised to direct six weeks of camp at Black Rock where I had been director the previous summer. I loved to keep the youth busy with hiking, swimming, relay races and scavenger hunts. The various activities helped them concentrate and prepare for the evening message. It was a privilege to challenge these youth to catch a vision of what it means to live a joyful Christian life and see how relevant Scripture can be, even though it was written hundreds of years ago.

After our summer at Camp Black Rock, we found an apartment near Eastern Mennonite Seminary campus, where I could walk to classes for my final year. Helen drove to her job at the Virginia Mennonite Home and, later, to her work in private homes. Our tiny apartment included a bathroom with only a toilet and washbowl and the privilege of using the landlady's bathtub once a week. Rent was $30 a month plus the cost of heat, which totaled $30 for the year. Occasionally on Friday evening Helen and I, along with David and Carol Garber, and Wilmer and Lois Harman went to Howard Johnson's Restaurant for their "All You Can Eat Fish Fry." I confess, I was guilty of eating more than my stomach appreciated.

PASTOR, SMITHVILLE MENNONITE CHURCH/ BIRTH OF OUR SONS

1961-1969

A few weeks before my graduation from seminary, we received a call to candidate as pastor for Smithville Mennonite Church in Ohio, southwest of Akron. The congregation had recently built a beautiful A-frame church, with an auditorium capacity of more than 200, plus a social room, Sunday school rooms and large pastor's study. It was intimidating and exciting at the same time.

I was extremely conscious of my stuttering problem. However, to my surprise, in what I consider one of the greatest miracles of my life, I learned that their former pastor had a speech impediment. We took this as a clear sign that God was calling us here and after further discernment accepted their invitation to begin after serving the summer at Camp Black Rock.

Home in Smithville

In Smithville, we rented a spacious apartment from the former pastor. The second day after we moved in, I met the youth group at a member's home, where we played croquet and enjoyed refreshments. Within a few weeks, I invited anyone who desired to accept Jesus and be baptized to come to the baptism class. What a thrill to baptize a dozen junior high and high school youth.

One year later, I made an appointment to meet with each one individually, only to discover that some were not sure about their salvation. I was embarrassed to think that perhaps I did not make the plan of salvation clear. From that point on, I tried to make sure I presented the plan of salvation as clear as possible and then check to see if they truly understood. I gave greater emphasis to the meaning of the steps of repentance, confession, belief and obedience:

Repent: Jesus said, "Unless you repent, you too will all perish." (Luke 13:3-5).

Confess: "If we confess our sins, he is faithful and just and will forgive us our sins and purify us from all unrighteousness." (1 John 1:9).

Believe: "Whoever believes in the Son has eternal life, but whoever rejects the Son will not see life, for God's wrath remains on them." (John 3:36). The Amplified Bible clarifies *believe* as "has faith in, clings to, relies on" Jesus.

Obey: Jesus said, "If you love me, keep my commands." (John 14:15).

Our Earliest Years Together

In our apartment, we enjoyed opening our home each month—rotating by inviting families based on the birthday month of the head of each household. This way we enjoyed more intimate fellowship with the entire congregation of 175 people. This helped us learn everyone's names as we played games and enjoyed the delicious food Helen prepared.

When we began our ministry in Smithville, Helen was only 20 and I was 24. We didn't know anyone when we arrived, but with Helen's special love for older people, she immediately felt comfortable spending time with them, as well as the younger ones. At times she accompanied me on my monthly visits to the nursing home. This way, she won the hearts and respect of everyone.

She also contributed her talent of flower arranging for our congregation to enjoy—taking her turn tending to the fresh flowers we placed at the front of the church each Sunday.

Helen worked nights as a nurse aid in one of the local hospitals and later part-time as a receptionist for a local doctor. She enjoyed meeting people and using her gift of encouragement. Perhaps it is best to say that Helen's main job was to be my prayer warrior and coach. She has always been with me heart and soul; my work was her work.

Throughout our married life, I depended on her prayer support and wisdom. When congregations called me to be their pastor, they got two for the price of one.

During my ministry, especially in the early years, I asked Helen to listen to my messages before I preached them. Her frequent response was, "Can't you tell it instead of reading it?" I worked and prayed to be more spontaneous, but it seems that is one prayer the Lord has not fully answered.

I am conscious, though, that unless the Holy Spirit takes the spoken words to the heart of the listeners, they are just empty words. Peter reminds me of the gravity of preaching: "If anyone speaks, they should do so as one who speaks the very words of God." (1 Peter 4:11). I'm sure that is why my messages and books are saturated with Scripture.

Learning How to Pastor

Each spring and fall, our congregation held a weeklong revival. For our Sunday morning prayer time during the revival, I announced that we would pray at 5:30 a.m. and at 7 a.m. I gave two options, knowing that we had several farm families in our church. When only one woman came at 5:30 and her husband came at 7, I realized that I had been over zealous and presumptuous. I had not learned to wait on the Lord for His Holy Spirit's direction before I announced the times. (John 10:3, 27). Also, I had not checked with my elders to hear their advice.

Blind 90-year-old Katie Kurtz lived at the Rittman Nursing Home. When I learned she had suffered a stroke, I went to visit. As I walked down the hall to her room, I heard her humming a hymn, as she usually did. I said, "Good morning, Katie. I understand you had a stroke." She immediately responded, "Oh, I am so glad it was on the left side, I can still feed myself." What a wonderful testimony. I pray that I will have her response when tragedies strike.

A Scary Storm

On another day, I traveled with Ralph, a church member and commercial potato grower, who frequently flew to check on his crop in

Pennsylvania. We landed in grass fields beside the potatoes. After checking the crop, we took off and were ready to head home when we encountered an unexpected thunderstorm. We couldn't fly around it. We couldn't fly above it either, because the air became too thin for our small plane. Lord, Jesus! Help us!

Eventually, we descended through the storm. Thank God the storm cleared just enough to see a spot of grass we could land on. Immediately, a jeep appeared and out jumped military officers. We had landed on a military base near Pittsburgh. After questioning us and giving us fuel, they sent us on our way. Praise God for His protection.

My First Wedding

Levi and Ella Yoder requested that I marry them—in what would be the first of more than 125 weddings I would perform during my pastoral ministry. Twenty-some years later, I performed the wedding ceremony for their daughter, Marilyn. My wedding messages were more than 10-minute homilies. I always spoke about Jesus being the center of the home for a marriage to be successful. I think Paul's advice, "Woe to me if I do not preach the Gospel," (I Corinthians 9:16) applies to wedding messages as well as Sunday morning sermons.

One year, through many of my community contacts, I officiated at three successive funerals for men in their 30s—none of whom had attended our church. One was killed in a motorcycle accident, another died of a drug overdose and another died from cancer. The widow of one of the men starting coming with her boys to church and Summer Bible School, until they moved out of the community. Fortunately, many in the congregation went the extra mile to include them in their circle of friends. Many congregations do not offer this gift of friendship.

Frequently, throughout my pastoral ministry, Helen and I invited new people we met into our home for a meal, to enable us to get to know them, share the Gospel and introduce them to our church life.

Economic Disparities – A Challenge

We frequently brought people to church who did not own a car. I brought a family to church who were living on public assistance. He had a minimum-wage job because of his limited ability; she cared for their 6-year-old son. At the time, Smithville was a typical Mennonite congregation of hardworking individuals with good-paying jobs. We tried to show love, support and care, but I regret that we never conquered the economic and cultural differences between us and this family, and they did not stay.

We faced the same challenges Jesus' brother James presented in James 2:1-13. In the New Testament, the rich and poor lived side by side. Today, when we get a promotion, we usually move to a neighborhood with less crime and better schools. This separates us from the homeless and those with limited resources. I regret that since we moved to Landis Homes, a retirement center, we no longer know the name of a homeless person.

Joyful Addition

Eighteen months after we moved to Smithville, our first child, Scott, was born. The nurse said to Helen, "I'll always remember the look of pure joy on your face when you saw your baby the first time."

Since I was never around babies, I kept saying to Helen, "Is this normal?" about everything Scott did. Helen, on the other hand, was completely at home, having cared for several nieces and nephews over the years, as well as helped mothers with little children.

After renting for two years, we purchased a new, small, three-bedroom house, with a full basement and single-car garage, for $13,500. We were close enough to Smithville Mennonite Church to see the church from our dining room window. I made a room in the basement for my study. We planted a large garden.

Family Pain

People often called Helen with their concerns when they could not contact me at the church study. Because of Helen's caring, sensitive heart, people's concerns weighed on her.

Helen lived with continual arthritic pain. Because of back pain, she saw a chiropractor for treatment. One day she visited him twice, because of the severe pain. He overtreated her, and she had to call a medical doctor for pain medication. That evening her body went into violent spasms. The ambulance arrived, fastened her to a gurney and sped to the hospital, sirens blaring.

Even after her return, Helen felt exhausted physically and mentally; she had difficulty walking and was on partial bedrest. Some people brought us meals, but others continued to call her with their problems as they had before. Instead of being a help to me, Helen felt she was a hindrance to the ministry. She felt the need to get away.

Helen chose outpatient care at a Christian psychiatric center in Elkhart, Indiana, while she stayed in a private home for a week. During that time, Scott spent time at Jack and Martha's home who had a daughter just a few years older and two school-age sons.

After Helen returned home, she followed up with group therapy in nearby Wooster. She enjoyed these sessions, finding them helpful. Following her final session, the counselor asked her if she expected to be greater than Jesus. Helen was shocked at his question. But then the counselor continued, pointing out how Jesus wasn't able to please everyone.

Helen knew that she tended to be a people pleaser. So the counselor's wisdom hit home, and Helen gained a lot from those sessions. In an unexpected benefit, some church members who learned of her experience began to question the stigma surrounding psychiatric care. One woman said, "If Helen can go for help, maybe I can, too."

We were soon looking forward to the birth of our second child, whom we named Jon Chester—after both grandfathers. Helen hemorrhaged soon after she came home from the hospital and had to be rehospitalized for several days. We were grateful for Orpha Hartzler, an elder's wife, who gladly accepted our newborn son into her home and lovingly cared for him.

Meanwhile, Scott stayed at the home of our church secretary, Lodema Hartzler, where he had a great time. Lodema told us how Scott would pick up all his toys before leaving her house to return home. She was amazed at his diligence in following through what he had been taught at home.

From early childhood, Scott loved to build with Legos. When he stacked blocks, we were sure they would fall over but he amazed us with his dexterity. As he grew older, he talked about wanting to build big things. Today he is project engineer for a large bridge building company and travels extensively, including foreign countries. Far more importantly he is taking Jesus wherever he goes.

Over the years, we never had trouble deciding where to go on vacation. Each summer and at Christmas or New Year's, we traveled to Lancaster County to visit with our families. Since our homes were only 4 miles apart, we easily spent time with both families. If we visited over a Sunday, I was often asked to preach at Habacker or another church.

Ministerium

The local pastors in Smithville met monthly and enjoyed great spiritual encouragement. In some of the community ministeriums in my 50-plus years of pastoral ministry, the conversation hasn't risen much beyond golf scores, to my great disappointment.

At the Wayne County Mennonite ministers' meeting at Crown Hill Mennonite, I was the youngest among the 20 pastors. Different pastors had left the ministry. I remember praying for God to give me many years of ministry. That was 50-some years ago. God answered that prayer beyond my expectations.

One fellow minister in particular was a definite encouragement to me. Although raised Jewish, Frank Sturpe accepted Christ as a teen. When his father discovered that Frank believed in Jesus, he threw Frank down the stairs and told him never to return.

The Jewish community even held a funeral for Frank and placed a grave marker in the cemetery. Jesus' words were real to Frank: "Blessed are you when people insult you, persecute you and falsely say all kinds of evil against you because of me. Rejoice and be glad, because great is your reward in heaven." (Matthew 5:11-12).

An Unbalanced Life

Because my church board wanted me to give strict account of how I used my time, I kept track of my pastoral visits. One year they totaled 818. This meant I was robbing my wife and sons of their time with dad. I regretted this unbalanced life and had to sincerely apologize for my behavior.

Unfortunately, I didn't learn my lesson. My bishop was too busy to hold me accountable for neglecting my family responsibilities. How I thank God for Helen, who was a wonderful mother and often a substitute father. Many wives would not have put up with a husband who too often put the church ahead of the family.

I was like Martha, whom Jesus said was concerned about many things but Mary chose the better or best thing: intimacy with Jesus (Luke 10:41-42).

The apostle Paul also made it clear that Christians' one goal in life is to run toward God and press in to him:

> "I want to know Christ—yes, to know the power of his resurrection and participation in his sufferings, becoming like him in his death, and so somehow, attaining to the resurrection from the dead. Not that I have already obtained all this, or have already arrived at my goal, but I press on to take hold of that for what Christ Jesus took hold of me. Brothers and sisters, I do not consider myself yet to have taken hold of it. But one thing I do: Forgetting what is behind and straining toward what is ahead, I press on toward the goal to win the prize for which God has called me heavenward in Christ Jesus (Philippians 3:10-14).
>
> "When Paul says, 'somehow, attaining to the resurrection" he was not implying uncertainty or doubt. He was unsure of the way that he would meet God, whether by execution or by natural death. He did not doubt that he would be raised, but attainment of it was within God's power and not his own. Just as Christ was exalted after his resurrection, so we will one day share Christ's glory (Revelation 22:1-7). His goal is to know Christ, to be like Christ, and to be all Christ has in mind for him. This goal absorbs all Paul's energy." (Life Application Bible notes.)

People especially enjoyed my pastoral visits when I took the family with me. On one occasion, Helen and I visited a lady whose home was filled with antiques. She had to move stacks of dishes so she could offer a place to sit. Although this lady never came to church, she usually gave a gift to the church and at times sent along a beautiful antique dish for Helen.

Church Growth and Ministry Opportunities

Praise God, attendance at Smithville Mennonite Church kept growing. When the students came home from college at break time, the auditorium—including the balcony—was filled with 220 or more attenders.

God has blessed me with the ability to notice and remember who is present on Sunday. When someone missed a service, we mailed a bulletin to them and prayed for them. After all, members belong to each other (Romans 12:5). Today it seems that far too many school activities are more important than church attendance.

Each summer while at Smithville I spent a week as director at Camp Luz, a Mennonite camp about 10 miles away near Kidron. For several years, I also served as youth sponsor for the Ohio Conference of the Mennonite Church—providing training to youth from 75 congregations and overseeing a four-page monthly newspaper.

I was amazed at the commitment of these youth to serve the Lord on the Youth Commission. We offered a yearly youth convention either in conjunction with the annual Christian Workers Conference or at Laurelville Mennonite Camp in Mt. Pleasant, Pennsylvania. We encouraged each church to host a Youth Bible Quiz Team. When I later resigned from pastoring Smithville Church, the conference leadership decided to employ a full-time conference youth minister.

For our church's Sunday evening programs, we often invited church members to present a particular topic. Thus, people grew in their knowledge of the Word and in leadership. For Wednesday evening Bible study, I prepared weekly prayer lists, often requesting prayer for people in the community whom I or others had contacted.

One of our elders led a monthly children's church during the regular church worship time. He prepared a special bulletin and invited the children to lead most everything except the "message" time.

In the '60s, Mennonites often discouraged the concept of small-group Bible studies; many believed this would lead to division in the church body. However, I encouraged a few young women with small babies to start their own Bible study, since evening services were especially difficult with their infants. God blessed this group, which continued for decades.

We held Summer Bible School in the mornings for two weeks every June. I remember one class for ninth and tenth graders that covered a chronological overview of the entire Old Testament; the next year we covered the New Testament. What an amazing understanding of biblical material these students had after those Summer Bible School classes.

Wooster College hosted a number of international students, and I would frequently bring them to the church for the worship service. They then came to our home for a meal. I learned from them that many international students never get invited by an American family for dinner in their home. This lack of hospitality is true even today. We found that hospitality is an effective way to share God's love. You can be a missionary for these students. Be bold and give it a try. You will be blessed!

The time we were at Smithville I often substituted as a schoolteacher to add to our income. I found those days quite challenging, especially when I taught at Boy's Village—a juvenile correctional school. When I asked one student to take his seat, he walked up to me and swung his fist but stopped just an inch or two from my face. I learned later that he had jumped from a second-story window because his mother was chasing him with a knife. That helped me better understand the pain he experienced.

Revival/Renewal Meetings

Most years I had the privilege of being the speaker for a revival series at another church. Other congregations also occasionally invited me to preach. At one of our own twice-yearly renewal meetings, the speaker said that if anyone has anything against another person, they should tell them. Following the service, Helen was surprised to find three middle-aged ladies wanted to talk to her about her shoulder-length cut hair.

Helen knew that cut hair was not unusual, except for older women. She shared with them that she was following her doctor's advice to cut her long, thick hair because of chronic neck pain. Evidently, the bishop had written an article in a church periodical relating cut hair to a harlot—an article that someone anonymously placed in our church mailbox.

Soon after that, when we were visiting family in Lancaster County, the pastor at Habacker Church invited me forward to participate in the worship service. But when the pastor saw Helen's shoulder-length hair, he quickly changed plans. At that time Habacker Church interpreted First Corinthians 11 quite literally. Today we believe it was because of the practice of prostitutes in Corinth to cut their hair it was forbidden for a woman to have cut hair.

We lived frugally. In our large garden, we raised vegetables for the summer, then we canned and froze food for the winter. Since we were struggling financially on our small monthly salary, we appreciated when some members placed a card with a $5 bill in our church mailbox at Christmastime.

In 1968, with much internal trepidation, I shared with the church board that we needed a raise in salary. They immediately gave me $1,000 and increased my salary. However, I felt so humiliated in asking that things never felt quite the same after that. Although I didn't understand it at the time, I can see now, looking back, that I was experiencing burnout.

I submitted my resignation and began to search for another pastorate.

WALDO MENNONITE CHURCH

1969-1973

After filling out the lengthy form for pastoral candidates, including what I believed concerning each aspect of our Mennonite Church doctrines, I submitted the application to the central office in Elkhart, Indiana. The conference minister in Illinois called concerning the need for a pastor at Waldo Mennonite in central Illinois, about 100 miles south of Chicago.

We had never been to that part of Illinois, where farms and houses often sit a mile apart. Many farms encompassed 640 acres, or one square mile. Thus, roads were laid out in square mile blocks, often without stop signs. When the corn grew tall, you could not see oncoming traffic as you approached an intersection.

Waldo Mennonite Church (now Prairie View Mennonite) stood at one such crossroads. The church building boasted an address in Gridley, but since the parsonage was located about 4 miles south in Flanagan, everyone referred to Waldo Church as being in Flanagan. Also, more people came to church from Flanagan than from Gridley.

The pastoral search committee invited me to be the pastor of this congregation of 175 attenders. Flanagan, a town of about 1,000 people, had three churches, a retirement home, grocery store, several restaurants, garage and hardware store, plus a school housing kindergarten through 12th grade.

Friendly Welcome

Flanagan welcomed us in July, 1969. Helen enjoyed taking Scott and Chet, then ages 6 and 2, to meet our neighbors, especially the many older persons in our church who lived throughout the town.

Ralph an elderly gentleman lived beside us. Helen and Chet took over a bouquet of flowers to celebrate his birthday shortly before Chet's third birthday. Walking back to our house, Chet remarked that old people like flowers for their birthday gifts but little boys don't like flowers for their birthdays.

In the basement of the parsonage, we found what looked like mouse droppings, especially around the canning shelves. After washing the shelves repeatedly, droppings soon appeared. We set traps, but to no avail. After we mentioned it to the trustee, he checked the area and determined they weren't droppings from mice but from water bugs. He sprayed the area, solving the problem.

Church activities included Sunday school and Sunday morning worship, Sunday evening worship and Wednesday evening Bible study. With Waldo Mennonite's attendance slowly declining, I suggested that we might merge with a General Conference Mennonite Church nearby that was smaller than Waldo, but the congregation was not ready for that. Years later after we left, attitudes changed and the merge occurred.

Shortly after we moved, one evening as we walked we looked up into the sky and said, "Hello" to Neil Armstrong as he took his first steps on the moon.

Four Funerals in Eight Days

In one period of eight days, I officiated at four funerals—all members of the congregation. In one case, the spouse died the same day her husband was buried. I was relieved when a neighbor pastor offered to preach the Sunday morning message. Not long after that I returned the favor by preaching for him when his baby daughter died.

At the other end of the spectrum, the college-age youth in our church all attended our church college in Goshen, Indiana. When they graduated, they moved to other communities where they could find work. In the four years I was at Waldo Mennonite, only one young person returned and eventually inherited his father's farm.

Everywhere, farm machinery was replacing farm laborers, so there were no jobs to be found. The surrounding population continued to decrease. Even though I did lots of visiting in the community, inviting people to church, it did not grow. Sometimes new families would attend, or a few who had dropped out returned, but they did not offset those who moved away. This meant I was pastoring a declining church.

I was not content. The Lord was teaching me a lesson I found difficult to accept: Not every church has to grow in numbers to be a healthy church. While understanding this intellectually, I didn't think that was God's will for me, especially while I was still young with a passion to reach people with the Good News.

Our community contained its share of colorful characters and sobering stories. One year, on my birthday, a distraught wife from our church called to say her angry husband was chasing her around the house with a knife. I quickly realized that violence isn't only in the big cities.

A Miser

Another man in our church community, I was told, never allowed anyone in his house. I purposely visited on a very cold, snowy day. He let me just inside the back door. Some said that he lived as a miser—rescuing food from a dumpster in back of a restaurant while owning several farms. When one of his farmhouses, barns or sheds needed repairs, he allowed it to deteriorate. It was up to the tenant to pay any expenses for repairs.

I tried to get him to help begin a Summer Bible School effort in Pontiac, but to no avail. Following his death, he left most of his estate to a local hospital. Jesus warned His disciples: "It is hard for someone who is rich to enter the kingdom of heaven." (Matthew 19:23).

When the Mennonite ministerium in Pontiac considered sponsoring a citywide evangelistic crusade, I suggested they contact Myron Augsburger, president of Eastern Mennonite College—named by *Time* magazine in 1969 as one of the five most influential "preachers of an active Gospel" in America. It was a joy for me to have Myron minister to the community on behalf of the many sponsoring local churches.

A New Development for the Denomination

I also served for two or three years as secretary of the Illinois Mennonite Conference. During that time, I helped set the stage for discussions about the ordination of women. Emma Richard had just returned from Japan, where she and her husband, Joe, had served as missionaries. Now, she was assisting her husband in pastoring Lombard Mennonite, a downtown Chicago congregation and member of Illinois Conference. In 1971, the congregation requested her ordination. After much prayer and looking at the many women in various leadership positions in the New Testament, we agreed to grant her ordination, which began to open the door for the denomination as a whole to consider the ordination of women.

Adoption of our Daughter

In the early '70s, drugs dominated the news. Peoria Child and Family Services was urging parents to adopt, since parents on drugs often couldn't care for their children. Helen had always wanted to adopt. When she was young, her dad had worked as superintendent at the Millersville Mennonite Children's home in Millersville, Pennsylvania. She'd lived at the home, watching her parents be "Dad and Mom Steffy" to 25-30 children. A few were orphans; others came from broken homes.

We talked to Scott and Chet about adopting a girl, and they thought it would be good to get a dog. We got both.

We submitted our application, went through several screening sessions and agreed to take a child, irrespective of race, although Helen preferred a little girl since we already had two boys. After evaluating our cultural context, Child and Family Services informed us that because Flanagan was a rural, basically nonintegrated community, they believed a black child might be a poor fit.

Several months after we submitted our original application in February 1971, Helen received a call to pick up our two-day-old daughter. I was at our monthly conference executive committee meeting in Blooming, 30 miles south, when Helen called me to come home immediately to bring our infant daughter home. Helen had already picked the name, Joy Noel. Chet was excited to go along with us to bring Noel home while Scott was in school.

The next days and months proved difficult, as Noel often cried and refused nourishment. Helen just held her close and prayed. Noel's bouts of crying seemed to stop sooner if Helen laid her in her crib instead of cradling her in her arms. The nurse in our congregation said the mother might have been on drugs, or maybe it was a "womb rejection."

After several months, things slowly changed and we all rejoiced, especially Helen, when Noel started to make eye contact and began to smile. Helen had prayed that a smile would mean God's love was flowing through her to Noel.

20 Degrees Below Zero

When I think of our four years in Illinois, I shiver. One winter it seemed the thermostat was stuck at 20 degrees below zero, continuously, for a whole week. At a number of funerals, the undertaker warned me to keep the graveside service short so no one would become frostbitten.

One time, I joined young people from another congregation on a weeklong Mennonite Disaster Service assignment in Biloxi, Mississippi, following a hurricane there. They rented a U-Haul truck to transport equipment and supplies to take with us, and I offered to sleep in a sleeping bag in the back of the closed-in truck. I basically missed a night of sleep going and coming, bouncing between Illinois and Mississippi. After working most of the week cleaning up downed pecan trees, I tried to preach during our Sunday morning at Waldo—without any sleep. When will I learn to say, "No"?

During harvest time in our community, farmers needed help to harvest corn and beans. For a few weeks each fall, I helped haul grain from the fields to the grain elevators. Also, to subsidize my income, I studied many long hours before driving to Chicago to get my Securities and Exchange Commission License, so I could sell stocks and bonds and life insurance. I never made much money but had a few good contacts with local farmers.

Rick May, a young man from our church volunteered to serve a year with Koinonia Farms in Americus, Georgia. Clarence Jordan, who wrote *The Cotton Patch Gospel*, had designed Koinonia Farms to welcome all people regardless of race. While Rick was working there, he died in a farm accident, crushed between a tractor and wagon. The death of this well-loved 24-year-old man was a blow to our church community.

I continued to have a passion to reach people for Jesus. Knowing that our local population was sparse and declining, I asked the Lord to please free me to move to where the people were more plentiful. My Mennonite Conference minister asked if I couldn't feel sufficient satisfaction in nurturing those in the congregation. I didn't answer him. I wanted to see more fruit for my labors.

NORTHSIDE MENNONITE CHURCH

1973-1983

When we learned of a pastoral need at Northside Mennonite Church in Lima, Ohio (population 50,0000), Helen's response was, "You'll have plenty of people to visit." In a prime location at 1318 N. Main Street, the church's attractive brick building was large enough to include a day care with 100 children and a large outdoor play space.

People called Lima "Little Chicago" due to its high crime rate tied to alcohol consumption and drugs. A large auto manufacturing facility with 5,000 employees dominated the city's economy. Several Northside Mennonite Church members worked there. The word was, you should never purchase a car that rolled off the inspection line on a Monday or Friday, because some of inspectors were drunk and passed most any vehicle, defects or not.

Northside Mennonite Church had started as the Lima Mission of Ohio Conference. Two years before we arrived, the previous pastor had fallen into sexual misconduct, so an interim pastor was holding things together.

As our family prepared to move from Illinois to Ohio, Helen took 2-year-old Noel to spend time with Helen's parents for a few days. I then drove the U-Haul truck with Scott, 10 and Chet, 6. The boys were fascinated to be riding in the big truck.

Learning to Rejoice in Pain

During Helen's time in Pennsylvania, God met her in a new way by giving her a prayer language in which to praise Him. In her pain and weakness, God was so real to her. As Paul says, God is made strong in our weakness (II Corinthians 12:10). She was learning to rejoice in the Lord regardless of her pain level, unaware of what was about to happen.

Within a few days of our family being together, Helen was hospitalized. She describes her experience in the following words:

Caught Between Principalities and Powers

> "There is no heaven or hell, and even if by chance there is, we'd be better off in hell. Besides—" Jessica continued flippantly, "hell's fire would warm our backs: instant heat packs."
>
> "Thank God, there is no suffering in heaven," I countered. "God promises His children a new body, perfect in every way."
>
> We lay in a dark green hospital room at the end of a long hall, far from the nurse's station. Jessica, my roommate, occupied the other bed. She lay in pain, the weights of traction hanging from her bed. Swirls of smoke circled her head as she nervously chain-smoked, a lit cigarette between her fingers and another still smoking in the ash tray. The TV blared from her speaker as the nurse adjusted the traction for my back.
>
> Cursing her back pain, Jessica let the nurse know what she could do with the damn traction apparatus. Immobilized in bed, neither of us could leave the room or escape each other's presence. I felt I was billeted in the anteroom of hell.
>
> *Lord, help me!* I cried out to God. *Stay close to me. I need your healing touch. Give me your peace—mine is gone. Channel your love for Jessica through me. May she see You alive in me.*
>
> My mind wandered back over the past weeks, trying to see if there was any way I could have avoided this hospital stay.

Living with the chronic pain of arthritis and its recurring flare-ups plus caring for our three active kids, ages 2 through 10, was a daily challenge for me. Recently, our family had moved from a rural pastorate in Illinois to the city of Lima, Ohio. My husband, Dave, was immediately caught up in the many responsibilities of a new pastorate while I unpacked and set up housekeeping, attempting to recreate "home" in our present setting.

Before moving to Ohio, I was admitted to Mayo Clinic while seeking a solution for a chronic back condition that at times immobilized me. Following a week of extensive testing, I was given pain medication and a list of "don'ts" restricting my activity. The physician's parting words, "You need to learn to live with your condition. In time, you'll probably need a wheelchair," was not the answer I was seeking.

My thoughts drifted back to our move to Ohio. I knew it would be a Herculean task in my condition to manage setting up housekeeping, finding time to do my back exercises, laundry, meal preparations, and the myriad details of adjusting to a new pastorate. Wearing my back brace and taking frequent bed rests, I unpacked boxes attempting to get the house in order, but my pain level kept escalating. I missed my Illinois physicians who were familiar with my condition. Seeking God's guidance and recommendations from my church family, I found a physician willing to accept new patients.

I lay in the car, my back brace holding me together, as Dave drove me to the physician's office. The reception area of the office was crowded. Since sitting was nearly impossible for me, I walked next door to the library while Dave waited for my turn to see the physician.

This library included a lending art gallery. Gazing at various paintings, I tried to concentrate on remaining upright and trying to block out my apprehension concerning the new-to-me physician. The librarian approached me, saying, "Pardon me, but I couldn't help noticing the way you are walking. My husband wears a back brace. Do you have a back problem, too?"

She gave me the name of two top neurosurgeons in the city. "You need to be referred by a doctor," she cautioned. "The neurosurgeons are immensely busy. Appointments need to be made months in advance."

I returned to the physician's office, where the doctor examined me and suggested a simple manipulation to help relieve some of the pain. I protested saying, "Don't twist my back." He ignored me, proceeding with the manipulating anyway. My pain intensified. I sobbed, petrified at being unable to straighten my body. God, help me! I was in more pain now than when I had walked in the office. Within an hour, the physician admitted me to the hospital.

Sedated with medication and secured in traction, I was surprised to hear the physician say he would have two neurosurgeons examine me in the morning. Yes, the very two neurosurgeons the librarian had recommended only a few hours ago. Surely God's ways are beyond understanding.

Would this be God's way of healing me? I longed to be able to live without pain, to carry out the many ideas in my head that often needed to be curtailed or at least scaled down to my present abilities. I had sought help from various medical clinics, chiropractors and faith healers. Many persons graciously remembered me in their prayers. Throughout the years of struggling with pain, Jesus became my life—my reason for living.

I found comfort in God's Word and identified with the words of the psalmist. At times, my heart, too, was bowed low in despair; but God always rescued me. I rejoiced in God's love for me. Yet, I longed to be a doer—to "do" great things for God. God said, "I want you to 'be'—allow me to live through you."

Lying in traction, my body exhausted with pain, I longed to fall asleep. The stale, lingering cigarette smoke-filled room coupled with my pain medication induced a throbbing headache. I needed peace and quiet to relax. Jessica needed noise and cigarettes. Her TV was on continually, the sound grating on my nerves. She, too, was in pain, restlessly smoking one cigarette after another. The smoke nauseated me. Moving to another room was no option; no other beds were available.

I shared my faith in God with Jessica. She didn't mind if I talked about God but became very nervous and, at times, angry when I mentioned Jesus' name. Jessica wanted no part of God with His supposed caring. She was in pain and in traction—no god came to her aid. I treasured the Word of God stored in my heart and meditated on its promises.

Jessica shared her belief in reincarnation, stating she could prove it by her own experience. She reasoned, "I must have lived somewhere in Africa in another lifetime. I often have terrifying dreams of being chased by black people throwing spears at me."

She seemed angry with everyone. Jessica complained when the nurse arrived to care for our needs and cursed them after they left. I didn't blame the nurses for avoiding our room. I longed to escape, too!

Circumstances remained the same. The TV vied with Jessica's constant talking. Maybe today another room would be available. Yet, as I talked to God, I sensed I was to stay where He had placed me. It was as if God said to me, "I placed you in this room in traction for a reason. Are you willing to stay and carry out my plans?"

Late at night the nurse told Jessica to turn off the TV. She refused. I asked to have the curtain drawn around my bed to block the TV screen, but it couldn't block out the noise. Jessica was totally involved in a war film, cursing and laughing as she watched persons being tortured—their bodies grotesquely mutilated. She seemed personally involved in the torture. Her hellish delight in the horror repelled me.

Exhausted and desperate for sleep, I rang the night nurse, requesting sleeping medication. No sleeping medication was ordered, but she could give me an injection for pain. The late movie ended; quietness settled over our room

My nightmare was just beginning, however. Within 10 minutes, intense pain built in my chest. I couldn't breathe. The nurse kept saying, "Relax! Relax!" Desperate for relief, my body seemed to be trying to turn itself inside out. Relaxing was impossible. My body no longer obeyed me.

The battle raged within. Exhausted from fighting for every breath, my body contorted into a seemingly impossible position. Here all was warm, dark and serenely quiet. Ah, peace at last. Is that what it's like to die? What a contrast to the intense struggle that waged war within me. Then, ever so slowly, I became aware of my body taking in oxygen.

I lay in bed amazed to be alive, my physical body at peace. The night nurse checked in on me before going home. "You really gave us a scare last night," she said, "You are allergic to Talwin. *Never* take it again!" Leaving the room, she pulled back the curtain separating our hospital beds.

Jessica looked at me strangely. "You're alive," she stammered. "I knew you were dying last night. I saw you dead. No one has ever come alive that I have seen dead," she emphatically declared. "How can you be alive?"

Trying to find a more comfortable position, I listened as Jessica talked about her supernatural powers. As a young girl, she was punished for revealing the death of a relative before word was received concerning their death. "Several times I've experienced a knowing. My friends don't want to hear about it, as they are afraid." Jessica laughed as she said, "I don't cause the deaths, I just supernaturally know about them."

She was fascinated with the power she possessed and desired to delve deeper into its mysteries.

Jessica seemed unable to speak without using God's name in a derisive fashion. "You must be a very god-conscious person," I said. Startled by my statement, she declared she was her own god.

Looking around the room as if to check its security, she continued, "One day a great shaft of light entered my body. It was a great spiritual feeling; I'll never forget. I'm always working to improve my power and control. Yet," she commented sadly, "this desire has cost me many friends."

In a few days, I was released to return home and finish

recuperating. The specialist's parting advice sounded familiar: "Learn to live with chronic pain, exercise but don't overdo."

I was thankful to be able to leave the hospital and return home with family. Yet my heart was burdened for Jessica, who remained in traction. God had answered my prayer in giving me His love for her.

At home that evening I shared some of the strange happenings in my hospital room with my husband. He listened. With much feeling, he softly replied, "You roomed with an angel of light. Jessica is possessed by evil coming to her in disguise as an angel of light. Thank God for His constant protection over you."

Ephesians 6:10-12 says, "Be strong in the Lord and in His mighty power. Put on the full armor of God, so that you can take your stand against the devil's schemes. For our struggle is not against flesh and blood, but against … the powers of this dark world and against the spiritual forces of evil in the heavenly realms."

Together, Dave and I thanked God for His faithfulness and protection. I had been in the midst of battle, too weak to be aware of all its consequences. Satan desired my life. I was no match for him, being physically weakened after days of severe pain, a violent allergic reaction of medication and immobilized in traction. God fought my battles for me!

I walked through the valley of the shadow of death, yet I never walked alone. God was with me, guiding me each step of the way. Satan said, "DEATH"—Jessica saw it. Jesus said, "LIFE" and conquered death for me.

The devil's most effective weapon is to have people believe he doesn't exist. Jesus and the apostles, especially Paul, cast out numerous demons. When people struggle to overcome anger, resentment, addictions with alcohol, drugs or immoral sexual passions, we need to discern if demonic forces lie behind those destructive habits. I believe that terrorist activity and mass shootings that are occurring most every day in our cities and even too often in schools illustrate Satan's activity. Jesus said to the unbelieving Pharisees, "You belong to your father, the devil, and you want to carry out your father's desires. ... He is a liar and the father of lies." (John 8:44).

On one of my first pastoral visits, a member of our congregation said, "You better be strong, or some of these people will shred you to pieces. They can be vicious." The apostle Paul once wrote that he fought beasts in Ephesus (I Corinthians 15:32), which commentators believe referred to strong opposition or evil spirits. What were we getting into?

Making Connections

We lived about 3 miles from church. Families with children surrounded us on every side, and community children gravitated to our place—drawn not only by our children but also by the adjacent vacant lot. The lot's apple and pear trees served as ammunition, even though we told them the fruit was for eating, not for throwing at each other.

The parents of a nearby family both worked, giving their children free run of the community. Another mother informed us that her child was being treated unfairly; she seemed to think it was our responsibility to keep the neighborhood children in line. Our children enjoyed playing with the neighbor kids but also occasionally liked getting a break from them all.

Witnessing to Our Neighbors

I made pamphlets and invited the neighbors to church. Helen had befriended the neighbor diagonally across the street, and after several months she said to Helen, "When I heard that a preacher was moving in, I was angry." She told Helen, "Someone had knocked on her door and asked if she was a Christian. She said she didn't know. He told her she was going to hell, but Helen, you are different. No matter what I say you just accept me." Helen kept praying for wisdom to know what and when to bring Jesus into the conversation. She felt the Holy Spirit check her each time. Not long after that, the neighbor and her boyfriend asked me to marry them. They came to church from time to time.

Years later, when we moved to plant a church in Florida, they traveled many miles to visit us. The husband said, "My wife just needs to spend some time with Helen." She found that Helen's love brought emotional and spiritual healing. We have kept contact with them over the past nearly 50 years.

We kept an ash tray handy in our home, because several friends and church members were chain-smokers. We wouldn't think of asking them to not smoke, because smoking was an accepted part of life in that community. We saw this as the least we could do, if it helped bring people to Jesus. When they left the house, however, we threw open the doors and windows to air out the house. Helen especially suffered because the smoke created headaches.

A peeping tom was believed to be in the neighborhood. Once our neighbor saw him looking in our bedroom window. He grabbed his gun and came running to our house but the Peeping Tom escaped.

A Wonderful Surprise

One day, the phone rang and the caller conveyed an emergency: Her husband had been "wrestling" with their young son as they often did before the school bus came. But this time, the son fell on his head, twisting his neck. He was paralyzed over much of his right side. When they arrived at the hospital, X-rays revealed his neck was broken. Surgery was scheduled for noon, and the mother of the boy, a member of our church, was asking for prayer.

We sent out a request on our prayer chain. Later, the mother told us that when they were preparing to operate, one doctor insisted they needed more X-rays—at which point they discovered nothing broken. Praise God for His healing power! The boy went home later that same day, healed!

With our three small children we decided to move. When a neighbor, a real estate agent, asked what price we wanted Helen gave her what I thought was a ridiculously high figure, yet the agent accepted. God was in the business of blessing us.

We immediately found a house three miles northeast on North Cable Road, the same distance from church but on a country road. There was a house alongside our property. A family with a son Scott's age were our close neighbors. Within a few weeks I installed a basketball hoop, which occupied many Sunday afternoons along with building a relationship with our next-door neighbor.

The large backyard was excellent for playing kickball. Saturday mornings I often assisted Chet with the *Grit* newspaper route in Elida. On weekdays I got the children off to school because Helen left early to work at our church day-care. I had a short prayer with the children before they boarded the school bus. I had shared with the children that it is often the church kids who test your faith. You expect the kids of the world to behave in ungodly ways so you have your guard up. But when church kids who claim to be Christians swear, cheat, lie, drink, or laugh at dirty jokes you are tempted to think: If they can do that, I guess it's ok.

Yearly Summer Vacation

Often before going on vacation to Pennsylvania, I would entertain the family with my "boisterous silly falsetto voice." They never did learn to appreciate my "talent." Noel was concerned that the neighbors might hear my "beautiful music" and suggest I see a psychiatrist.

For our summer vacation we visited our parents in Pennsylvania. A number of years when our children were growing up, Faith and her husband John Nissley invited us to go with them to the "Blue Hilton," a hunting cabin in Tioga County in northern Pennsylvania. This was a time for our children to bond with Faith and John as we hiked, played games, spotted wildlife, sang songs around the campfire and prayed together.

Tragedy

Chet enjoyed having his friend Albert come to our house. Chet had Albert to our house for a sleepover. Albert left early Saturday morning to accompany his older brother to deliver ice. Tragically, they were in an accident that morning and both boys were killed. At the church funeral the high school boys carried the caskets, shoulders heaving with grief.

Standing by the casket, tears in her eyes and sobbing gently, Albert's mother looked at Helen and said, "You have your son. I have only a picture of mine." Life can be short. In First Samuel 20:3 Jonathan said, "There is only one step between me and death." Jesus reminds us, "He is the resurrection and the life. The ones who believe in me will live, even though they die." (John 11:25). Occasionally Chet stopped in to see Albert's mother when he delivered the *Grit* papers. She greatly appreciated his visits.

Helen created many special moments for our family with her culinary skills. Some Saturdays when we didn't need to hurry, Helen made a special breakfast. Chet loved pancakes and enjoyed helping mix the batter. We would sit down together and sing Scott's favorite breakfast song:

"Father we thank Thee for the night
And for the pleasant morning light
For rest and food and loving care
And all that makes the world so fair
Help us to do the things we should
To be to others kind and good
In all we do in work or play
To love Thee better day by day. Amen."

Springtime brought the humble dandelions across our lawn. When the children were younger they enjoyed picking them and bringing them to Helen. She graciously accepted their gift and arranged them in a vase, giving them a place of honor on the kitchen table. Seeing dandelions reminds her of the pleasure on the children's faces at her delight of their gift.

We thanked God for the large backyard with huge hickory nut trees. At the backside of the property was a storage shed where we stored a lawn mower and garden tools. On two sides fields bordered our property. Beside the shed was a large sunny area for a garden and a strawberry bed.

Adding a Family Room

Since we had no basement, we were praying about the possibility of adding a family room on the back of the house. At that time Helen read Isaiah 54:2, "Enlarge your house; build an addition; spread out your home!" (NLT). This encouraged us to explore this possibility.

A pastor friend who worked part-time as a builder built a 20 x 20-foot family room attached to our house. It was a great place to play ping-pong on the table I had built in my high school shop class. In winter we would build a fire in the stove and often play ping-pong. The boys soon learned to beat dad. The table worked well to help Scott put his 5,200-piece puzzle together. In the summer we made home-made ice cream on our cement patio, taking turns turning the crank until the ice cream became firm. For some reason the home-made ice cream always tasted better than the bought ones.

Helen's parents and sisters came to visit us from Pennsylvania. On one occasion Grandpa Steffy built a treehouse in the mammoth hickory tree for the children to enjoy. It also came to be my prayer closet and place to prepare sermons.

A guard-rail plant was known as the dirtiest place in Lima to work. Workers changed clothes before going home. I approached the manager and asked if I could bring my lunch and eat in the lunchroom to relate to the men and perhaps invite them to church. After doing this a few times I felt my attempts were not effective and gave it up.

The Best Use of Your Time

On my way to visit people I often had to stop at a railroad crossing waiting for the train to pass. I kept a New Testament handy to read, so I was not tempted to be frustrated with the long wait on the train. One stop proved to be quite profitable. Romans 5:1-2 came alive to me. "Since we have been justified by faith, we have peace with God through our Lord Jesus Christ, through whom we have gained access by faith into His grace in which we now stand." I never need to struggle or work to have peace because I am standing in His grace. What a promise!

I commend to you, keep God's Word with you at all times. Get a small pocket New Testament and keep it in your pocket or purse. Keep one in the glove compartment of your car, in your bathroom, on your coffee table. Don't be without God's Word. You never know when you will find yourself with idle moments. Like David, "Store God's word in your heart that you will not sin." (Psalm 119:11).

Rocky Mountain Trip: July 19 – August 3, 1977

Our August 1977 summer vacation was a once-in-a-lifetime experience. Faith and John invited us to go with them in their new van to the Rocky Mountains. After driving 500 miles we slept in Wisconsin. For 500 miles we saw signs to Wall Drug. Chet said, "After all these signs it better be good." We weren't too impressed! It wasn't long before we could see the Rocky Mountains in the west. At Mt. Rushmore in South Dakota, we were amazed at the 60-foot-high carvings of presidents: George Washington, Thomas Jefferson, Theodore Roosevelt and Abraham Lincoln. We waited for two hours listening to music until the sky darkened. As the lights were shown, features of the presidents' faces seem to stand out in detail against the darkness of the night sky.

Entering Montana, we watched as two cowboys guided a large herd of cattle across the highway to another pasture. We stopped along the road to make our supper. Chet hiked up the mountain. When he turned, he started to run but couldn't get stopped. He screamed! John and I locked hands and caught him. If he would have broken through, he would have fallen down a huge cleft beside the highway and been seriously injured. How we thank God for sparing us this tragedy.

In Wyoming we crossed two rivers named: The Dead Horse and the Crazy Women. Helen wondered who named the rivers and what was the story behind them. Driving through Montana we stopped to pick ten pounds of large delicious cherries for 25 cents a pound.

We were impressed with all the animals we saw in the Canadian Rockies. We enjoyed God's creation seeing two eagles and heard the tapping of the woodpeckers. A coyote hurried across the road in front of us. We watched as six mountain goats with five kids came down out of the mountains, walking toward the road. They were shedding their coats and looked like rugged hill billies. They probably were coming for water in the stream on the other side of the road. Walking along Lake Louise we were impressed with the beauty of the greenish-blue color of the water. Its color is due to suspended particles of glacier silt. Getting up early, John and I watched a bear upsetting garbage cans close to our cabin. I guess it was his breakfast time.

Heading east, Helen especially enjoyed sitting in the Hot Springs in British Columbia. They were better for her back than the hot towel treatments I had been giving her.

I read *The Cross and The Switchblade* to the children during the long distances between stops. Six-year-old petite Noel often sat in the back on a blanket-covered board placed on top of the suitcases. She could enjoy the passing scenery or snuggle down for a little nap. She delighted in this special place made just for her.

Old Faithful Geyser in Wyoming dazzled us with its powerful burst of steam and water. We drove past the badlands of South Dakota and stopped at the Corn Palace. After traveling more than 600 miles we were relieved to arrive at 4635 N. Cable Road, Elida, Ohio.

Sunday Night Drive-in Church

On Sunday evenings during the summer, we had drive-in church. Our quartet sang, I preached a short message and then we showed a film as people sat in their cars. This went well for a couple summers until the husband of one of our members who despised the fact that his wife's lifestyle had changed since she became a Christian reported us to the police because the film audio disturbed the peace. We were forced to discontinue our film ministry. Jesus said, "I did not come to bring peace, but a sword. For I have come to turn a man against his father, a daughter against her mother... a man enemies will be the members of his own household." (Matthew 10:34-36).

In order to subsidize our income, I bought an apartment house in Lima with four units as well as a single dwelling on an adjoining street. The strain of collecting rent, of keeping the units repaired—especially a leaking flat roof—and the high rate of turnover with tenants was a drain on my physical and spiritual energy. The final decision to sell came when I learned that a neighbor was threatening to take me to court for allowing renters to make excessive noise at their drug parties. With what profit there was for all my work we supported a little girl in India. God was gracious to me. I was able to recover my investment when I sold the units following this four-year experiment. My three children were relieved as they didn't enjoy helping to clean up after renters moved out.

Thriving Day-care

Northside Mennonite had a thriving day-care center with 150 children enrolled, some were part-time. Most of the employees were members of the congregation. At enrollment it was explicitly stated that Tuesday was Bible story day. This way if they were opposed, they knew not to send their child on Tuesdays.

When parents saw fifty children sleeping in the auditorium, they often commented that they had difficulty getting their two children to sleep and were amazed we had fifty quietly sleeping. A staff that exemplified God's peace in their heart and life contributed greatly to this atmosphere of peace. Jesus said, "Peace I leave with you, my peace I give you, I do not give to you as the world gives." (John 14:27).

Helen has always enjoyed children. Listening to their stories is a delight to her. She taught the older two- and three-year-old class at day-care. Sharing stories with the children and telling them how precious they are to Jesus made her day. Children seem to have a delightful sense of God. Their faith is special. Jesus said, "Unless we become like children, we cannot see the Kingdom of God." (Matthew 18:3).

One spring morning Helen cut one hundred daffodils from our flower beds and gave them to the children to give to their parents. Their excitement and pleasure showed on their faces as they cried out, "Thank you!" Oh, to be like children who enjoy the simple things of life.

One morning the director told Helen that Sara may need extra love today. The parents were away the previous evening and left the older children in charge. Her half-brother threatened to kill Sara last night. She was the only child of the new husband's wife and the stepbrother was jealous. When the other stepchildren heard his threats, they quickly called the grandmother to take Sara. Sara said, "I knew Jesus wouldn't let him hurt me. My teacher says, 'Jesus loves me. God cares for me.'"

Many of our children were from the huge Catholic Church across the street. Each spring the children gave a program for the parents, which packed the auditorium as the well-disciplined children preformed. In the '70s it seemed children and adults were hospitalized more frequently than today. Seldom did a day go by that I was not visiting someone in the hospital. When children from the day-care were hospitalized, I visited. This resulted in a number of families coming to Northside Church.

Occasionally there were persons with Mennonite background who moved into the area. Unless they had a passion for missions, they usually went to the more traditional Mennonite Churches in the country. Northside had people from all walks of life. One man, an extravert, was a heavy drinker for 26 years. He got saved and brought his extended family who took Jesus' command to be ambassadors seriously. I went with him to visit people he had contacted. He told me not go alone to the bar to witness unless he was along. What a thrill it was to welcome these persons who had little understanding of the Christian faith. The church was the salt and light Jesus intended it to be. Praise God! (Matthew 5:14-16).

The denomination published a yearbook with statistics of each conference as well as national membership. My heart wept as I read the new yearbook figures. We were a body of approximately 100,000 people but were growing less than one percent a year here at home. Where is our passion for the Lost? Does it enter our minds that our neighbors are lost?

Non-Christian Friends

I had many friends who were non-Christians. One lady was living with her boyfriend who was continually getting drunk. She wanted to get him out of the house. I thought I was doing her a favor when an elder and I moved him and a few belongings to a room in the YMCA. But the next morning she was irate at me for moving him. I hope I learned my lesson.

Don't ever excuse yourself for saying you don't know people who need Jesus. Whenever we see a "real estate" or "for rent" sign, or a U-Haul, stop and welcome the new family. If appropriate, invite them to church. Helen met a new family by saying, "I have been praying for you." With surprise the new mover said, "But you didn't know who was moving here." Helen said, "God did." They were Christians but she never thought to pray for people who were moving in. Pray for people moving in. Stop and discover where they are on their faith journey.

One week we had a "Family Life" theme. The guest speaker was a psychologist who introduced us to the chorus that reverberates in my mind to this day:

"I'm covered over with the robe of righteousness;
Jesus gives to me. (gives to me).
I'm covered over with the precious blood of Jesus
and he lives in me. (lives in me).
What a joy it is to know my heavenly Father

loves me so and gives to me my Jesus.
And when he looks at me, he sees not what
I use to be but he sees Jesus."

That simple chorus, should cause us to walk around with a spring in our step, a smile on our face and a song in our hearts.

About this time a book that impacted my life was Watchman Nee's, *A Normal Christian Life.* He wrote a dozen or more books and later died in a Chinese prison because of his faith in Christ. I preached through the book of Romans using many of his interpretations and illustrations.

Historic Blizzard of 1978

The worst blizzard in Ohio history came in January 1978. At one corner of our ranch house the 70-mph winds blew drifts as high as the roof. Scott and Chet stepped from the drift onto the roof. Snow blew in through the louvers on the overhang of the house. I shoveled the snow into the garage. Scott and Chet shoveled it outside. They built tunnels in the drift in the backyard. Fifty-one people died. Fortunately, it came at night when schools were closed. Snowmobiles transported hospital workers. Farmers poured their milk on the ground. When roads started to open, I took milk my farmer neighbor gave me to people in Lima.

I had been serving as Chair of the Evangelism Commission of Ohio Conference, which was designed to encourage church planting and revitalize congregations that were not growing. Approximately half of the funds contributed to conference work were channeled through this Commission. The funds were mainly used to subsidize mission congregation throughout the state.

We had opened up a number of abandoned churches in southern Ohio that had closed because of the poor economic conditions and declining attendance. The Commission gave subsidy for pastoral support. This proved to be successful in several situations largely because of the sacrificial dedication of the pastoral couple. A few others eventually closed for lack of interest from those in the community.

Radio Ministry

Two or three times a year the local Christian radio station, WTGN, featured our church as "The Church of the Week." The worship service was broadcast plus a 15-minute weekday morning devotional followed by a time for people to call in their prayer requests. I enjoyed this opportunity and received many affirmations. One year when the station manager couldn't find anyone to take the Christmas week, I filled in. That week 116 calls came in for prayer. I loved praying for people's needs. When WTGN began a Christian TV station I had the privilege of being their first speaker for their weekly featured church.

Scott's industrial arts teacher was impressed with Scott's ability and recommended him for after-school hours employment to the John Deere plant. Scott soon spotted a flaw in one of their design drawings. His employer was quite impressed. The next summer he worked at the Bowman Cabinet Shop just a stone's throw from our house.

Helen and I had gone to the three-week Clyde Narramore School of Pastoral Care in Los Angeles. I had been exploring the possibility of enrolling in the Doctor of Ministry program at Ashland Theological Seminary, affiliated with the Brethren Church. This was a conjoint doctoral program with Methesco Seminary (Methodist) and Capital Seminary (Lutheran). With the encouragement of the Narramore School I enrolled and found the courses challenging. What helped me greatly was our church secretary, Marlene Sizemore. This angel insisted that she take my assigned papers home with her and typed the final draft for me. After taking the doctoral examination, which qualified students to continue in the program, I had the highest grade of the six candidates. As a struggling student in much of my schooling, God blessed me. He is fantastic! I was able to do more than I could imagine. (Ephesians 3:20-21).

Sometimes God Says It With Flowers

The following article was written by Helen.

"At a women's meeting several women were wearing corsages. The guest speaker focused on God's great love. Before the offering was taken, we were told to seek God to know what He desires us to give in the offering. As I listened, I thought I heard God saying He wanted the corsage I was wearing. *Did I hear correctly? I can't just place it in the offering basket.* The meeting was over. The corsage still pinned on me.

As I was walking to the car, I thought, *did I hear God wrong?* Then I noticed Anna standing beside the car waiting for the woman who brought her to the meeting. Anna was on welfare with seemingly multitudes of problems. Our church had assisted her and her husband at various times. I had helped her with food and tried to teach her some simple basics of homemaking.

Tears streaming down her cheeks, she angrily said, "I had to get out of that meeting. All that God talk didn't help me any!" I listened as she continued her complaint. Slowly I took off my corsage and pinned it on her. "It no longer belongs to me." I said, "God asked me for my corsage during the offering and He wants you to have it. It's a sign of His great love for you."

On the way home I thought, *what will I tell Dave as this was a special gift from him?* I told him what happened and his comment was, "What will her husband say, getting another woman's corsage?"

I admit I did feel foolish, yet I knew that was what I was to do. The corsage was special to me as I love flowers, especially carnations. Dave's corsages were few and far between. Many times that week I prayed that whenever Anna and her husband were close to the corsage they would feel especially loved.

The next Sunday Anna met me after church. She said, "This is going to sound crazy. I put the corsage in the refrigerator so it would last longer. The carnations are so pretty and fragrant. It's the weirdest thing. All week my husband and I kept going to the refrigerator just to see the corsage. Whenever we were close to it, we felt as if we were being loved. The presence of love was so strong we just had to experience it over and over."

I embraced her and said, "That's not weird. You see, I wanted you to know God loves you. I asked God that whenever you were near the corsage you would feel especially loved. He was simply answering my prayers for you and your husband. Sometime God says His love through flowers."

Helen enjoys landscaping. Linda, a former member came to visit us in Lima. When she saw Helen's flowerbeds she said, "You are beautifying America one place at a time." As we were traveling together Helen pointed out a huge mulch pile. Linda laughed, "You're the only person I know who envies somebody's mulch pile."

Charismatic Renewal

The next big step in the doctoral program required that I have a project involving the congregation. My five elders assured me that everything was going well in our congregation and approved my proposed project entitled: Developing Koinonia in an Urban Congregation.

I had been attending the Full Gospel Christian Businessmen's meetings enjoying their enthusiasm and exuberant worship. The Charismatic movement was making inroads into our surrounding communities. Women's Aglow, an arm of the Full Gospel movement asked me to serve as their pastor advisor, which I accepted.

Helen continued to live with continual pain from arthritis and lower back pain. Friends who were deeply involved in the charismatic renewal strongly encouraged her to be anointed. She had been prayed over, hands laid on, and anointed before. She would say, I am walking with Jesus and desire my healing but Jesus has not healed me to this point. To make matters worse some implied that it was her lack of faith that she wasn't healed. They were like Job's comforters causing more pain than comfort. (Job 16:2-5 and 16-21).

Charismatic theology emphasizes comfort and prosperity. However, Paul writes, "We glory in our sufferings, because we know that suffering produces perseverance, perseverance, character; and character, hope." (Romans 5:3-4).

I believe God heals but from the Scriptures it is evident physical healing is not for everyone. Jesus often healed all who came to Him. Other times, as in John 5 where a great number of disabled people used to lie—the blind, the lame, the paralyzed—He only healed one who was an invalid for thirty-eight years. Paul was ill when he came to

Galicia. The Galatians treated him as if he were an angel (Galatians 4:13-14). Timothy was frequently sick (I Timothy 5:23). Paul left Trophimus ill at Miletus (II Timothy 4:19). Epaphroditus almost died (Philippians 2:25-30). Jesus said we are to visit the sick (Matthew 25). Other times he said we are to heal the sick (Luke 10:8).

Sometimes Jesus heals us physically. But sometimes He works an even greater miracle—He heals us spiritually. He gives us the Holy Spirit's strength and courage to bear up under life's sufferings. Sometimes He removes the pain, and sometimes He does an even greater work of giving us the strength to endure the pain with joy. We know the suffering of this life is not worth comparing to the joy that awaits us in heaven (Romans 8:17). God can heal our bodies, and He can heal our souls.

Joseph didn't understand why he was enslaved in Egypt. Moses didn't understand why he had to spend forty years in the desert. Joshua didn't understand the flooded Jordan River and fortified city of Jericho. Daniel didn't understand the lion's den, or Paul his thorn in the flesh, or John his Isle of Patmos prison. It was all part of God's larger plan. One day God will wipe away all pain, sickness and suffering (Revelation 21:4).

Be Careful How You Pray

One brother who had experienced several persons being healed was taken to the aged mother of one of our members. In his prayer for her healing, it was reported that he demanded any demonic power to be cast out. To think that her mother might have a demon exasperated my member so that anything I said or did that could be interpreted as relating to the chiasmatic renewal was greatly upsetting.

A Huge Surprise

It was customary for the practice of many Mennonite congregations to vote every three years if they desired their pastor to continue another term. After a long, nearly three-hour meeting in the church basement for my congregational vote, while I cared for their children in the auditorium, the meeting finally ended. The Conference Minister said he never experienced a meeting like this. He could not say anything I needed to change but my vote was not high enough that I felt I should continue here. I learned that the individual who could not tolerate anything resembling the Charismatic movement felt that I was getting too involved. The Holy Spirit used this individual to move us into a new phase in our ministry. (The practice of voting every three years has basically been discontinued throughout the denomination.)

It's an understatement to say that my poor vote was a shock to us, especially since my elders assured me things were going well in the congregation and I was given a green light to proceed with my doctrinal studies. Helen and I didn't sleep much that night. Early the next morning one of my elders who had always supported me knocked on our door. He was awake most of the night. He said he voted against me to get me out of this frustrating situation. We had no idea what lay ahead.

Saying "Goodbye" to Northside was painful. In one sense it was the best ten years of our life. Lives were transformed. We had baptized many adults and youth. Church attendance had grown significantly. The day-care was an effective witness in the city. I had served as Chair of the Evangelism Commission of the Ohio Mennonite Conference for several years. I was in the midst of my doctoral program.

We continued to live on Cable Road and pastor for the school year. We had the house for sale for months but were not successful in finding a buyer. By the time we set to move we had found renters. They moved in. There was sulfur in our well water. They complained and threatened to move so after we put up with sulfur water for eight years, we invested in a water purifier rather than lose our renters. After three years the roof was showing signs of needing new shingles. My father-in-law came from Pennsylvania one long weekend and put on new shingles as I helped him. Renting a house 120 miles away was frustrating. After four years of renting the house, "For Sale" signs went up. We finally got the property off our hands.

PEACE MENNONITE CHURCH

1983-1990

For some time, Don and Erma Taylor were calling the Evangelism Commission to plant a church in Elyria, a city of nearly 60,000 west of Cleveland. We were unable to find a church planter despite a full-page advertisement on the cover of our conference magazine. The Evangelism Commission greatly encouraged our family to plant this church.

With the blessing of Northside Church, I drove the more than 100 miles from Lima to Elyria for several monthly meetings to pull together a core group. As always Helen was praying for my safety driving these back roads late at night. She kept praying for God's will to be done. Unless the Lord builds the house, our labor is in vain (Psalm 127:1).

Housing Miracle

Helen and I chose to rent since we couldn't sell our house in Lima and also we did not know the community or where the church would locate. We chose a ranch house just south of Elyria and north of Grafton in the village of Brentwood. We agreed on an occupancy date. Less than a week before we were to move the landlord decided not to rent after all. What should we do? Helen told her fellow teachers and staff at the day-care, "God will provide a way. We are moving as planned."

A few days later we received a call that another property diagonally a few houses up the same street just became available for rent. We moved on the day we had planned to a nicer place than we originally chose. Out of the hundreds of streets in Elyria, God had picked this street and house for us. Our motto is, "Let the supernatural become natural." This was clearly God's will for us.

Soon after we moved Helen invited the neighbor women to our home so we could meet them. Interestingly, two neighbors who lived diagonally across from each other for 17 years had never met. Invite your neighbors to your backyard for games and dessert so they can meet each other. As Christians we show love by building relationships.

Noel became friends with Terra across the street. Terra was babysitting and brought Oliver, her stepbrother, the preschool boy to our house to visit with Noel. He saw the creche and asked about it. He, like millions of children, had never heard the Christmas story. Helen enjoyed telling the true story of Christmas.

One night Noel gave a frantic yell. Apparently, a bat came down the chimney and was flying around in her room. I finally caught the critter. Noel never did learn to appreciate bats.

Group Formation

We met in Donald and Erma's living room with the attendance in the teens including their three children. They made a few contacts with persons leaving a small church planting that decided to close. Goshen and Eastern Mennonite College gave me the names, addresses and phone numbers of alumni that moved to Lorain County after graduating from their colleges. A few showed interest, but no one indicated a solid commitment.

We needed a name for the group in order to open a checking account. We agreed on Peace Mennonite Church. Looking back this was a mistake. The Mennonite name was not well known in Lorain County. Those who knew about Mennonites often associated them with Amish. In other areas where Mennonites are well known the name is less offensive. It's best to stay away from denominational names. One can still uphold biblical beliefs and make disciples while using a more generic name.

Answers to Prayer

I learned of a family with two children who lived south of Wellington about 15 miles away. They graduated from the Mennonite College in Bluffton, Ohio. I went to visit them and as she said, it was as if God sent me. Another answer to prayer! Their family, with their two little children was a boost to our morale since we had no young children. The next few years we enjoyed going to their farm Sunday afternoons for fellowship and cookouts.

I sent out letters to families using the reverse phone directory to find their name, address and phone numbers. A reverse phone directory lists streets with each house number and name of those who live there. A week after I sent the letters introducing our church plant, I called their home to see if they received the letter and had any interest.

Frank and Janet Sabo indicated some interest since Frank, years ago in Pennsylvania had attended a Mennonite Brethren Church. They came. The following Sunday they brought their son and his wife. When I learned that Frank played a guitar and his son Mark, a mandolin, I had them play the next Sunday. I never heard the hymn "Holy, Holy, Holy," being played with a mandolin but everyone enjoyed their efforts, furthermore the mandolin gave an atmosphere of lively worship, which I felt we needed.

Frank proved to be an evangelist. Over the next few years, he brought twenty-eight people to church. Most were relatives. Not all of them became faithful followers of Jesus but Frank was a definite encouragement to all of us. Every Wednesday evening, we met in Frank and Janet's living room for Bible study and prayer. Tuesday evenings we met in our living room. John, one of our members worked in a nursing home and arranged for several persons in wheelchairs to participate in our Bible studies.

We were growing. It was necessary to find a larger facility. We began a building fund almost from the outset but were far from thinking of buying a property. After a diligent search we finally found the Nord Center, a rehab facility in south Lorain just off Route 2. We met there for more than two years.

Christ the King School

Since there was no youth group in our church plant, the Taylors recommended we enroll our children Noel, grade 7, and Chet, grade 11, in Christ the King Christian School in North Olmstead, Ohio. Scott was a junior at Goshen College. Parents were expected to participate in Christ the King School programs to offset the tuition cost.

I served as substitute teacher. I also taught a "Survey of the Old and New Testaments" for ministerial students in Christ the King University as well as two non-credit short-term classes.

The administration of Christ the King Church asked me to serve on their Board of Regents for Christ the King University. The University was growing rapidly. Seventy pastors had indicated they would help support this effort, which was now a megachurch. They had a vision for expanding their university and building a center for senior citizens. After serving on the Board of Regents for two years, I felt led to resign. Several months later I learned that the pastor and his associate were both involved in sexual misconduct. What a blessing it was not to be directly involved in that painful situation.

In order to complete the requirements for my Doctor of Ministry degree at Ashland Theological Seminary I needed a project that involved the congregation. The project I began at Northside in Lima was "Developing Koinonia in an Urban Church." This proved to be problematic. Paul commands us to love each other more and more (I Thessalonians 4:10-11). How could I measure love and fellowship? With a sense of relief, I gave up this theme.

Instead, I chose "Discovering and Developing Spiritual Gifts for Church Planting." I wrote a curriculum describing each of the thirty-one gifts I found in the Bible. Seventeen persons, including two high school youth, came to a 13-session class on Sunday mornings before church. I designed a tool to discover what they knew about spiritual gifts and what gifts they thought they might have. I recorded these findings before the class sessions. After this three-month class I interviewed each student to discern what they had learned and how they might utilize their gifts. I wrote my findings for each student and defended my study before three seminary professors. This project was helpful to me to understand people as they functioned in church. I was the first Mennonite to participate in Ashland's doctoral program.

Celebration Time

In 1985 we had a great celebration at our house for the men in our family. Chet graduated from high school looking forward to going to Goshen College in the fall, Scott graduated from college anticipating his studies at Purdue University in civil engineering. I had just received my doctoral degree looking forward to helping people grow in the understanding and use of their gifts.

25th Wedding Anniversary

The children invited our friends and surprised us on our 25th wedding anniversary, with a beautiful cake and all the trimmings. They took care of all the details and we were totally surprised as people arrived at our house. The children gave us a lawn swing, which brought back many memories of sitting on the lawn swing at the back porch of Helen's parents' home. In the cool of the evening, we had many intimate talks swinging back and forth getting to know each other, looking forward to all God would have for us in the future.

During the summer, Scott worked for the highway department in the hot sun repaving roads. Chet and Noel worked for an upscale caterer. Noel also worked in restaurants. She chose to go to Center Christian High School in Kidron for her junior and senior year.

Painsville Church Plant

We discovered there were two families with Mennonite background that had moved to Painsville, northeast of Cleveland. After making contact I met with them and a few of their friends to explore the possibility of beginning a church. Cleveland has snowy and icy roads most of the winter. Helen prayed for my safety and the emerging group as I traveled 75 miles there once a month to lay the foundation for a church.

The Evangelism Commission called a church planter who in a few months developed a group of about 60 people. On Easter Sunday there were over 100 persons present. However, shortly after that the pastor decided to move in order for his children to be enrolled in a particular Christian school. He helped the attenders find another church fellowship. I can't put into words the great disappointment this was for me and our Conference Evangelism Commission.

Growing Brings Challenges

Having outgrown the Nord Center we moved to a Baptist School that had closed its doors. Being unable to find a building to purchase we turned to looking for land to build. An eleven-acre plot of ground was available on West Ridge Road, south of the Open-Door Bible Church in northwest Elyria.

Paul Showalter, a lifetime builder, and Nancy, his wife, retired early and were volunteering through the Elkhart (Indiana) Mission Board to assist emerging churches with their building projects. They agreed to help us. We put out a plea to our sister congregations for both funds and volunteer labor. Peace Mennonite had raised sufficient funds to purchase the property. Over the next months contributions from our sister churches in Ohio Conference came to $65,000. More importantly, several churches promised they would be providing labor for various aspects of our building, especially cement work, plumbing and heating, roofing, bricklaying and siding. One person donated all the cabinets.

Paul with his administrative skills did an excellent job of coordinating these workers. As frequently happens it took longer than anticipated to finish the building. This meant we were forced to rent the local YMCA for three months for our worship services before we could receive our occupancy permit.

A tragedy was soon to occur. Paul and Nancy moved to Oregon to assist in building a church there. While Paul was close to the peak of the building he was constructing he fell and died immediately. The church had lost a faithful servant. Only God can explain to us in eternity the reason for this sudden removal of His dedicated servant. When we get to heaven God promises, "I shall know fully, even as I am fully known." (I Corinthians 13:12). God will clear up for us any mysteries we need to know.

My Parents

My parents sold the farm to our neighbor John Harnish in 1976 and moved to Ivy Drive near East Petersburg. They enjoyed several years there attending Landisville Mennonite Church. Mother had been strongly urging Dad for them to move to Landis Homes, a retirement community near Lititz. Faith arranged for them to move. In the meantime, Mother fell and broke her hip. That meant she needed skilled care and was not able to stay in the same room with Dad. Shortly thereafter at age 85 she suffered a fatal stoke. Dad lived two more years. While I had made several trips from Ohio it was a great blessing that Faith could frequently stop by and visit with my parents. During two summers Chet lived with Helen's parents in Millersville and worked at Turkey Hill Dairy in Conestoga. Chet often spent evenings listening to my dad share stories from his life. This was a blessing for me as I was miles away in Ohio.

When my parents died, we came as a family for the funeral at Landisville Mennonite Church. They were buried in River Corner Mennonite Church Cemetery alongside my infant sister, Miriam.

Reaching People

While I was in the study in Peace Mennonite, our church sign caused Ray to stop. As a child Ray was dropped off Sunday mornings at a Mennonite church. Ray had been in Viet Nam and suffered emotional trauma as he held his buddies' mutilated bodies until they died. He was president of his motorcycle gang, "Hell's Angels." Ray and I developed a close friendship as he confessed his sins, and wept with horrific pain over his past experiences. I took Helen with me to meet his beautiful wife. Ray was extremely controlling. He forbid his wife to see her parents because they were not in favor of their marriage. She defied him and continued to visit them. In his fierce anger he hired a hit man to kill her. The hit man reported him to the police. Ray will die in prison. He pours out his heart to God in repentance. God judges fairly and justly. I hope to visit with Ray in heaven. Yes, God's love reaches Ray's heart if he is truly repentant.

As a little girl, Sue was terrified of her alcoholic father. Whenever he came home, she would hide in the closet. As an adult she gave her life to Christ. Her emotionally crippled life began to heal. Life was not an easy road for Sue, but she became a leader. She is reaching her family and friends for the Lord. Sue has made it a priority to reach people for Jesus. "Those who become Christians become new persons. They are not the same anymore, for the old life is gone. A new life has begun!" (II Corinthians 5:17 NLT).

Bob Bair, an architect for the local college related to our church. He and his wife, Aileen, felt a call for Bob to leave that position and enter full-time with the Bill Gothard Institute of Basic Life Ministries serving in Asia. Bob's life was often in danger as he ministered in restricted areas. God used him to equip hundreds of pastors throughout Asia in the late eighties and early nineties. They were a great encouragement to PMC.

There are trying times. Pete, his wife and son came to church. They seemed like a model family. He had a good position at the Cleveland International Airport. She played the piano for us and he became our Sunday School Superintendent. After some time, he withdrew to himself in quietness; and did not communicate. He packed his bags and was gone, leaving his wife and son without support. He'll never know the pain and heartbreak he caused.

Use Your Imagination

Can you imagine an Amish man working as an air traffic controller in a large airport? We had a family that came to church for a year or so. They home-schooled their children, dressed like Amish, lived pretty much like Amish but drove a car. They were a fine Christian family working in a high-tech position. God's love transcended our difference. We experienced joyful fellowship.

Another man came who also dressed like the Amish. He really chewed me out for not being more like the Amish and Mennonites are supposed to be from his perspective. After we moved, I learned he was living a double-faced life—professing to be one thing but living another. Paul writes in II Timothy 2:18, "Hymenaeus and Philetus have departed from the truth." It happens today. One Sunday he came in his jeep, parked in the church parking lot and out jumped a chicken. We never did catch the chicken. People make life challenging and interesting!

Helen's Challenges

Helen was living with pain. Mayo Clinic had told her years before she was headed for life in a wheelchair. She told the doctor, "I couldn't live without God." As the medical specialists checked over her records and X-rays, he said, "If I had a body like yours, I would be angry with God. I wouldn't be praising him." As Helen shared different times how she experienced God's presence and how He came through for her he said, "You're a billboard for God!"

Helen identifies and is encouraged by Paul's words when the Lord said to him: "My grace is sufficient for you, for my power is made perfect in weakness. Therefore, I will boast all the more gladly about my weakness, so that Christ's power may rest on me. That is why, for Christ's sake, I delight in weaknesses, ... for when I am weak then I am strong." (II Corinthians 12:9-10).

Transition Time

There were two young men in the congregation that had aspirations of being pastors. One was teaching public school for several years. He was disappointed with the liberal direction his denomination was taking and was participating in our church for over a year. The other young man was still in seminary but was proving himself by his diligent study and faithfulness to be an upcoming pastor.

We had been in Elyria seven years. I felt led to step aside in order for one of these two, to hopefully move into the pastorate here at PMC. After we moved, they chose the schoolteacher. What a joy it was to see the church prosper.

The congregation honored us with a two-hour time of sharing joyful experiences of people who came to know the Lord. Our fellowship had been rich. We laughed and cried as Frank and Mark Sabo sang a humorous song they had written about our ministry. Tears of joy for God's goodness ran down my cheeks as we gave our goodbyes.

In the years following our move, the church held its own for 15 years or so then began to decline especially during the Covid-19 pandemic, which resulted in the death of Lyle Troyer their leader. More recently they have asked the North Olmstead Evangelical Friends Church to assist the congregation. We pray and believe with great joy that this will bring new life to this congregation.

Marriages

Our family is growing. God gifted us with two daughters, Scott married Joy Burris on September 2, 1989, in Attica, Illinois. Three months later, December 16, Chet married Holly Miller on a cold snowy day in Walnut Creek, Ohio. Noel married Chad Warren, October 8, 2016, in a private ceremony.

CHURCH PLANTING IN NORTH PORT, FLORIDA

1990-1994

Southeast Mennonite Conference was calling for a church planter. We drove to Sarasota on the Gulf side and met with the search team. Noel had just graduated from high school and enrolled in Goshen College rather than move to Florida with us. We were empty nesters. Our car broke down on the way, which meant paying for unexpected car repairs and hotel bills.

The search team had decided that North Port, about 30 miles south of Sarasota, was the projected site where we were to focus. Since we could not find a house to rent in North Port, we settled in Port Charlotte just a few miles south of North Port. When we were cleaning out the asparagus ferns that had grown up around the back door, we found a nest of snakes. What a warm welcome!

Two families who were worshipping in a Mennonite Church in Sarasota agreed to be part of our core. I made the mistake of not insisting we have a pianist or guitarist or someone who could help lead the music. We met in our large living room for Bible studies. As usual I made fliers and went from house to house in both North Port and Port Charlotte.

For the first few months on Sundays, we met at the town park pavilion in North Port. This was not ideal because of the noise of people in the park and frequent rains.

Occasionally after a long hot day, Helen and I enjoyed walking across the long bridge over Peace River between Port Charlotte and Punta Gorda. I'm sure Andrew and Peter could have given the sailboat operators a few helpful hints to navigate their sailboats.

A church in North Port had built a social hall attached to their sanctuary with a covered walkway. They were declining in numbers with no children except occasional Sundays when their children came from out of town with grandchildren. We rented their social hall for our Sunday worship services.

Drugs

When a woman came to church I visited in her home. Her husband was not socialable so I didn't stay long. I encouraged him to come with his wife and then left. Several days after my visit, his wife called and informed me her husband was involved in a drug ring. She gave me the date and time when these men were to meet at their home. I was to call the police. When the time came, I drove by the house noticing extra cars not usually there. I called the police giving them the information I had. They didn't seem to be excited about my call.

The North Port City town fathers expected the city to grow rapidly. They had paved many miles of streets where building lots were laid out but not sold. We had been informed that at times planes would land on these empty streets, drop off their drugs to those who were hiding nearby and then take off before the police could arrive.

Testing Time

The mayor of North Port was an active Christian. I stopped at his place as I was going from house to house inviting people to church. In our conversation I had mentioned that I went to Eastern Mennonite College in Virginia. He gave me the name of a family he thought had some connection with the college. This family with three small children was a blessing. They came for several months but soon moved away because of a job opportunity.

As I was going house to house a woman was riding bicycle with her two young girls. After talking with them she encouraged us by coming on Sunday. Her husband came for a time but later lost interest.

After the first year we were encouraged as attendance was running in the forties. However, one of the two original families moved to Ohio. Others, including the family the mayor introduced left because of work opportunities. Ted and Beth and their two children decided that I was not following the church calendar year close enough so they left and returned to their more liturgical Lutheran Church. Our group was nearly cut in half. The Lord was testing our faith. I remember distinctly walking alone, going from house to house, praying and crying out to God for His wisdom to find those who would consider coming to help build this new fellowship. Hopes were dashed frequently as people would promise to come Sunday but not show. It was painful to go to my monthly support group meeting in Sarasota and report little progress.

I thank God that He will not allow us to be tested beyond what we can bare (I Corinthians 10:13). This was one of those times I had to claim His promise.

Wintertime was encouraging as people from the north came for vacation. A few of our friends, especially from churches I pastored, vacationed there and helped fill some empty chairs and participated when the offering plate was passed.

Grandchildren

Not long after we moved to Florida, Noel gave birth to our first grandchild, Dustin Miller, on March 4, 1991. Later she married the baby's father, Denny Miller. Their daughter, Katie, was born on December 2, 1993. Unfortunately it was a difficult marriage. For safety reasons for herself and the children she divorced Denny.

Chet and Holly served in Jamaica with Mennonite Central Committee. Their first child, Micah, arrived July 13, 1992. While Chet was in seminary in Elkhart, Indiana, their second child, Samuel, was born August 6, 1995. Scott and Joy's first child, Jonathan, was born in Homewood, Illinois, on June 28, 1993, followed by Jesse, on June 15, 1996. Later, when Chet and Holly moved to Maryland, Mary, our final grandchild was born on December 11, 1999.

God's Guarding Angel

After preaching I was traveling from North Port to meet my family in Lancaster County, Pennsylvania. It was two in the morning, raining cats and dogs and suddenly I saw this tractor trailer in front of me. I hit the brake and the car hydroplaned. It seemed to speed up. I yelled, "Jesus! Jesus! Jesus!" I heard a thud, instantly my car moved over missing the trailer by inches. God's guarding angel spared my life.

Since the majority of our people were from North Port we moved from Port Charlotte. We found a house with a pool. The backyard sloped along a river. I soon learned that a pool was not without its work in keeping it clean. The chlorine must be kept at just the right level. Helen really appreciated the pool for her arthritic joints. We had an exciting morning when Helen noticed a snake in the pool and yelled for me as she quickly left the pool.

I purchased a used dingy for $200 and enjoyed rowing up the river among the alligators, turtles and snakes. Frequently a large alligator laid by the water in our backyard sunning himself. Since we had a small dog, we had to keep him on a leash or he would have been devoured.

To subsidize my income, I obtained my real estate license and worked a few hours a week at the office. While I did make a few small sales I soon learned this was not my calling. Having my license, however, assisted me in hunting for land to build our church. We bought a plot near the projected center of North Port (3010 S. Sumter Blvd., North Port). I say projected center because much of North Port was undeveloped land laid out in streets. We erected a sign: Peace Church, and had our Easter Sunrise Service there. Now the church is renamed Peace Community Fellowship.

David Beachy, a retired builder, offered to help me purchase a house and fix it up to rent. We, especially David, put in many hours. It was disappointing in that the only profit I had was my portion of the real estate commission. Throughout my years God kept underscoring the fact my calling was to be a pastor – church planter. What I didn't realize—God was preparing me for future work but I had no idea what that might be.

A family from Venice was active in a large evangelical church. When they heard about our church plant they came to visit. They were pacifist, worshipping in a congregation that strongly promoted the military. They soon felt at home with us and were a definite boost to our group. Their musical talents were greatly appreciated. Others came and built the attendance up to the seventies.

Challenges

An individual was involved in inappropriate behavior. He confessed his sin to me and we felt sure things were forgiven and healed. However, our relationship was never quite the same after that.

At the same time one of our members, a schoolteacher, was beginning a Christian school and desired my help. This did not set well with a couple families who believed that Christian schools were actually a hinderance. Their belief was that our children should be in public school to give a Christian influence there. The upcoming school needed to have someone underwrite an insurance policy in case a child was injured and would sue the school. I felt I had cleared this with our leadership team. I had checked with the lawyer and he felt there was no problem for us to give our consent to this request.

Because of this, tension continued within the church. I met with the secretary of the Conference. After some agonizing prayer and discernment, Helen and I felt we needed to move on. We didn't want to split the church plant. Looking back, this was God's way of closing one door so He could open another that resulted in the highlight of our 50 years of pastoral ministry. After all these years we are still learning to trust the Lord.

We had no idea what the future might be. A fairly new attender at church called and encouraged me. Formerly he had a high position in the Jehovah Witness Church. When he accepted the Lord his entire family and friends deserted him. He said that he did not understand what is going on but God directed him to call and encourage us. He'll never know what an encouragement he was to Helen and me.

We explored via phone a few possibilities but did not feel any of these God had planned for us. We needed to sell our house. This time there were multiple complications over the next four years until it finally sold. God continues to teach us to cast our cares on Him.

FROM COTTAGE CITY TO CAPITAL CHRISTIAN

1994-2006

Cottage City Mennonite Church was located one mile east of Washington, D.C. The church was begun in the 1960s. It became the home of several young men who were classified as conscientious objectors. They believed followers of Jesus should not take up arms and enter the military. The congregation had prospered often with the help of Mennonite youth groups who came from Lancaster County, Pennsylvania, to deliver tracts and provide street meetings.

By 1994 however, the congregation had declined to forty-some. We flew to D.C. The open discussion with the congregation was vigorous. On our return flight Helen and I agreed this was not the place for us. Our dilemma was, how are we going to tell these hospitable people we are not coming. Throwing ourselves on God's mercy for His guidance, we felt led to change our minds and say yes to answer their call. It's only as we humble ourselves and say, "God, I want only what You want that we can hear His voice. If this is what You want, I am willing and ready to go." God gave us peace as we moved forward. Solomon admonishes, "Lean on, trust and be confident in the Lord with all your heart and mind, and do not rely on your own insight or understanding. In all your ways know, recognize and acknowledge Him, and He will direct and make straight and plain your paths." (Proverbs 3:5-6 AMP).

Our son Chet flew down from Elkhart to assist us in our move to Maryland. Lewis Good, the bishop and acting pastor was also a real estate agent. He found us a house to rent in Lanham, Maryland, directly across from a strip mall. Twenty-three stoplights were between our house and the church. Our neighbors stayed to themselves. Not long after we were there a neighbor came and said if the police come and ask questions just be quiet. Thank God the police never came. It was an adjustment for us to live in this context.

I was supported eighty percent. To make up for the other twenty I began working toward getting my Maryland real estate license. Just as in North Port, I learned I was not made for real estate.

Together Magazine

Cottage City Church distributed the *Together Magazine* from our Mennonite publishing press to the homes in the area. We designed a form in the magazine for people to submit their name and address if they would like a free turkey. Quite a few people had received free turkeys in previous years. Thirty families requested a turkey. The people gave me a warm welcome but when I mentioned about the possibility of coming to visit our church there was little interest.

Only one family came to church regularly from Cottage City. One or two single persons walked to church. No one came from D.C. located to the west of the church. Those who came to worship commuted from a distance. We were not a community church.

Spanish people were moving into Cottage City. It was clear to me we needed to make some drastic changes if we were to survive. Another family with children informed me that they would likely be leaving. I asked them to give me a year, after that if they felt they needed to leave, I would understand.

The Boldest Statement of My Life

I wrote a letter presenting three options for the elders to consider. Option one was to remain at the Cottage City building and die. This was the boldest statement of my life. Option two was to stay where we were and make some radical changes such as changing our worship style, using more contemporary music, perhaps build a gym and offer activities that the community people would appreciate and use. Option three was to move the congregation to a new location. One of the elder's wives when she read the paper said, "Don't let anyone see this."

After more prayer I felt I needed to move ahead by visiting each home. My first visit was on New Year's evening 1995. When I stated the reason for my visit their son, who recently graduated from high school said, "I've been telling mom and dad all along that's what we need to do." He'll never know what encouragement that was to me. As I visited families, I found people were open to the idea of moving to a new location. They were honest enough to face the reality that the church was in decline and would eventually close its doors unless we made a definite turnaround.

On April 1st at a congregational meeting, we decided unanimously—23 to 0—to move to a new location. What a miracle! We had no idea where. One person said, "If we can't grow here, how will we grow there?" Lewis Good and I checked dozens of places. Finally, one of our members who taught at Capitol College in Laurel suggested we check if we could rent their auditorium. The Sunday morning rental was $300 for the use of the auditorium and three classrooms.

Imagine a group of 45 people going to an auditorium ten miles away seating 337 people. Our first service in June had more people come from Cottage City than when they could walk across the street to the Cottage City Church. The one lady who came regularly from Cottage City when she heard we might move came to Helen and said, "I'll never get my husband to come. He only comes here when our daughter is in a program. He will never drive that distance to church." Helen replied, "I will pray. He will come." He came that first Sunday and has come ever since. As a member he is a good worker and supporter of Capital Christian Fellowship. People who hadn't invited anyone to church for years at Cottage City now became engaged and brought their friends.

We chose the name Capital Christian Fellowship (CCF), changing the "ol" to "al" since we met at Capitol College. We developed a worship team accompanied with piano, guitar, trombone and drums. I brought a woman and her children who were from Nigeria. I learned she had relatives who sometimes sang as a trio. We were thrilled by their singing and even more so by their testimony of God's deliverance in their persecution experiences.

Another Move

We bought a house just two miles from Capitol College in a community of four hundred homes. Within two weeks I had given invitations to each home, to worship and also to come to our home for a mid-week Bible study. As usual, Helen was praying as I walked and invited. If people gave any indication that they might give us a try I kept notes and returned a month later. For those not home I returned on a weekend or evening so I could hopefully touch base with them. It's a privilege to live in a nation where we can legally share the Good News. We have no idea how long we will have that privilege. The first Wednesday evening our neighbor came and brought another lady.

While Helen was in our front lawn a couple walked by walking their dog. Helen chatted with them and invited them to church. They said, "Sunday morning we take our dog to go swimming." Sadly, more and more Americans are finding many things are more important than church. David wrote: "The wicked shall be turned in hell and all the nations that forget God." (Psalm 9:17 KJV). Taking your dog swimming is not being wicked, but giving it priority over worshipping God is clearly wicked.

Patience

It was already past time to begin the wedding. The bride came to Helen and asked, "Where are the candles? Where I come from the church always provides the candles." Helen hurried home and thanked God as she found the white candles. She hurried back only to sit another hour. When the bridal couple was finally ready it was two hours and twenty minutes past the time to begin. The pianist asked me what to do. I suggested she just play the same music over and over. Working with people from a variety of countries and walks of life required grace and patience.

I received a call at midnight from a distressed wife. Her husband left the house in anger. I called Bishop Lew. We found him walking the streets in D.C. If the police would have seen him before we did it would not have been good. They were immigrants from Guyana. He was unable to get a job that adequately supported his wife and children. We helped him find a better job. With many hours of sharing God's love, they became active participants in church.

Leadership

A key to our growth was that every Friday morning the elders met from 6:30–8:30. We often met at Ruth Harnish Yoder's place.

Ruth was the daughter of John Harnish, my neighbor at Central Manor who gave me work to help put me through college. Ruth, an elder for many years, continues as one of the pillars of CCF. The agenda for elders' meetings was Scripture, discussion of how our new people were properly followed up and how they might be equipped to expand God's Kingdom. We prayed throughout the meeting. Even though at times we met in a restaurant our focus was not on physical food but on the spiritual. Unless the leaders of a church are willing to give sacrificial service it will not prosper. Later, as I did church consultation work, I could not persuade leadership teams to give that kind of time in prayer and in the Word—even though they were frustrated that their church was in decline.

I made sure every Sunday there was a person or several persons on the stage who were non-Caucasian. Having them up front made a clear statement that everyone was welcome and included. Because of our steady growth it wasn't long before we had more persons of color than Caucasians. The growth also enabled us to employee a part-time music worship leader.

Our head usher, Ray, oozed with graciousness. Being black he knew what it was not to be welcomed. As a young man he was a professional baseball player. Whenever they traveled in the South, he would have to enter a restaurant in the back and sit alone to eat. Ray organized a monthly block party to discuss any problems that arose between neighbors. Ray was a peacemaker (Matthew 5:9).

We always had prayer counselors in front of the auditorium for anyone to come forward for prayer after the service. Mindy poured out her heart to Helen and found forgiveness and healing for the several abortions. James writes, "Confess your sins to one another and pray for each other so that you may be healed." (James 5:16).

Multiplication

A couple and their son who were from Cameroon came. Soon others from Cameroon came. Daniel encouraged us with his memorization of the Book of Hebrews as well as other smaller New Testament letters. These people gave impetus to our emerging congregation. What a blessing! Another blessing was a lady college professor came and over the next two years brought several of her family and friends.

Three different times in Acts the leader of a household brought their whole household to Christ (Acts 16:15, 33, and 18:8).

A mixed couple came: He was Caucasian and she was black. We sang, "Whiter Than Snow." "Now wash me and I shall be whiter than snow." When I went to visit them, they were angry that I would allow this song to be song in our church. Even though our worship team consisted of mixed races and the music leader was in a mixed racial marriage they would not consider returning.

Hilda was a German woman who married a U.S. soldier during World War II. After the couple settled in the United States, her husband was promiscuous. He frequently brought women into their home and slept with them in another room. I told Hilda various times that God does not demand she stay there, she could leave. Her response was, "Where could I go? I can't live on the street."

Hilda raised her husband's children from these relationships. Although Hilda gave her life to Christ, she continues to struggle with a smoldering temper. I prayed with her many times as she talked about murdering her husband's girlfriends. Even though she lives in this hellish situation, Hilda continues to grow in her relationship with Jesus and has had a positive influence on her family and many others. For years a Bible study group met in her home, which I helped to lead.

A Delightful Surprise

We needed an assistant pastor. Chet and Holly and their two children, Micah and Sam, moved to northern Virginia for Chet's doctoral studies in international peacemaking at George Mason University. To our delight they came to CCF. One of the most surprising and delightful words to ever reach my ears was Chet saying to me, "Dad, I would like to be considered as a candidate for assistant pastor of CCF but I don't want to preach more than once a quarter." Everyone was delighted. The once-a-quarter request soon changed. Chet learned to enjoy preaching and we shared the pulpit the next five years they were with us.

One of our faithful sisters brought Alivia and her 6-year-old son to our church. Alivia had a managerial position in the Social Work Department with a salary of $80,000. Finances were a problem but she refused to change her style of living. She seldom washed dishes or clothing, instead she simply bought new clothes or took them to the dry cleaners. They ate carry-out meals. I never visited her but that the clothing was strewn across the floor and the sink and counters overflowed with soiled dishes. She heard the Word but did not do what the Word said. James 1:22, "Do not merely listen to the Word, and so deceive yourselves. Do what it says." Pastor Chet and I tried to help her but she was unwilling to change her lifestyle.

Discipleship Groups

Chet had done a tremendous job of getting the new people into twenty small discipleship groups. Small discipleship groups are the key to a healthy church. It doesn't matter when or where they meet but people who never meet with others will develop a warped theology. The seventeen "one-another" directives in the New Testament are not there just to take up space. To become healthy, mature disciples of Jesus we need the love and accountability of other Christians.

Helen and I tried to have these new people into our home. One Christmas she baked 116 dozen cookies for them to enjoy. Many said they didn't bake cookies and loaded paper plates to take home.

When I was sweeping some dirt that had accumulated on the floor at church several ladies saw me and immediately took the broom from me. They didn't want to see their pastor doing menial tasks. Jesus came to serve, not to be served (Mark 10:45). Serving is a privilege. We are to serve one another in love (Galatians 5:13). Whoever wants to be great must be your servant (Matthew 20:26).

School for Apostles

What a joy for Helen and me, after being away from Black Rock Camp to return for Eastern Mennonite Missions' yearly School for Apostles. We were the old ones among thirty or more younger couples and their many children. The speakers, mostly from urban centers, challenged us with their reports of transformed lives. We felt empowered and left with fresh energy to reach others for Jesus, and make disciples.

Roy had recently gone through a divorce. When he came to church I was impressed with his knowledge of the Bible. However, I soon discovered pornography controlled his life. Satan convinced him this was fine. I permitted him to come to church but made it clear he was not to talk about his "freedom." It wasn't long before I had to ask him not to return. He went to another church where he and the pastor became the best of friends. It's obvious why the American Church has lost the respect of many. Jesus said, "Blessed are the pure in heart, for they shall see God." (Matthew 5:8). One survey reveals that more than half the pastors in the U.S. admit to viewing porn at least monthly. Is it any wonder the nation is going downhill morally!

600 Phone Calls a Month

I contacted New Movers Evangelism, which provided the names, addresses and phone numbers of persons who moved into a given zip code. New Movers received their information through courthouse records. I subscribed to this service and for several years made 600 phone calls a month. Helen prayed and I would call, usually in the evening. I would say in one breath, "Good evening, I am Pastor Dave, from Capital Christian Fellowship, if you have found a church family that is wonderful, if you don't have a church would it be ok with you if I'd send you an invitation to come some Sunday to worship with us at Capital Christian." About one in four gave a positive answer.

I made note of anything they said that I might connect with them when I called back, as for example some said they couldn't come Sunday because they will be on vacation, or they couldn't come because one of their children is sick. A week or ten days later I would call and ask if they received my invitation or remembered talking with me. If they said yes, I asked if there was a possibility they might come some Sunday. About one in five said they would try to come some Sunday.

I'd often prayed with these people over the phone. If they did not come, I would call once a month for six months and then say, "I don't want to waste your time or mine. I will not call again unless you say it is ok for me to call." It was not uncommon for them to say it is ok for me to continue to call. This was possible because I had developed a friendship by praying over the phone for their children or whatever needs they had.

Summer Vacation

Now that our children had grown and married, we came together at the "Blue Hilton" again for a few days each summer. This was a time of building life-long memories with Scott & Joy and their children Jonathan and Jesse, and Chet & Holly and their three children Micah, Samuel and Mary, and Noel and her children Dustin and Katie. What a privilege it was to have the entire family of fifteen sit around the long table and enjoy the food Faith and John provided, listening to the children's chatter as well as the adult conversations.

We enjoyed hiking, wading in the cool mountain streams, skipping stones across the water and playing games. One year we sat on the hillside watching fireworks in Galton.

We looked forward to the early evenings spotting and counting the deer as we rode slowly through the hills and farmland. Around the campfire we enjoyed singing songs together sharing about our walks with the Lord and praying together. As the darkness descended the children had fun playing with the sparklers Aunt Joy provided, dancing and giggling as they excitedly waved them through the air. We slept well in the cool mountain air. Eventually John retired from the hunting club. It's been years since we have been at the cabin but fond memories linger.

Chet's Family Moves to South America

It was a joy to have Chet and Holly's family live nearby. We enjoyed having them in our home and babysitting the grandchildren. After more than five years with us, Chet and Holly felt the call to foreign work.

Mennonite Central Committee (MCC) was searching for someone with training in peacemaking for the Anabaptist congregations in Colombia, South America. Several Anabaptist groups had started work but with the violence and unrest they were eager to begin a conflict transformation center and were struggling to work together. Pastors were sometimes murdered but Chet and Holly felt God's clear call and moved forward with their three small children. Mary had joined their family in December of 1999. At critical times God spared his life and the life of their family. For a time, he walked to work a different time every day taking a different route so he would not be easily followed. At times they did not go out of the house for days.

Wedding in a Bar

Robert's father was a minister. But Robert eventually turned his back on the Lord and the church. After living through a painful divorce, he moved in with another woman. They lived together for several years. I visited them a number of times. Robert and his girlfriend opened their hearts to Jesus and started coming regularly to church. Several months later, at their insistence, I married them in a bar because they wanted all their old friends to witness their Christian marriage. They knew many of their friends would never come to church not even for the wedding. They served our Lord faithfully in church ministry: he on the worship team and she in the church kitchen. Robert returned to the bar, not to drink but to share Jesus with his buddies.

Another unusual experience; I was invited to a dowry party, which was a reenacting of the custom of auctioning the bride. Even though it was done in fun I had a difficult time appreciating this cultural practice, which was so opposite of the Christian principle of everyone being created equal in God's image. How can a child of God be auctioned? (I John 3:1).

Whenever a family member or friend died in Cameroon the people from Cameroon who came to CCF held a wake to honor the deceased. People brought food, gathered in a home, sat quietly, meditated, and went to the kitchen whenever they desired where there was plenty of food. Then about 11 p.m. I gave a Scriptural meditation. There was sharing and prayer. I stayed until midnight while most of the others continued meeting and sharing for another hour or two.

Another family were dedicated Christians and came faithfully to church but did not join the church. I visited with them and inquired about their hesitancy. They said that they can't seem to agree on a name for their two children when they are baptized. Would we take baptism more seriously if we had to be given a new name? God will give us a new name when we get to heaven, presumably our name will describe our character (Revelation 2:17).

For diversion I built a 10 x 12 shed in our backyard. Nearly all the materials, except the shingles, were salvaged from dumpsters sitting in building developments. The floor was constructed of 2 x 8's. I placed windows in all four side from windows I rescued from the dumpsters. The trusses were built with 2 x 4's. Noel loved to tease me about being a dumpster jumper. This was a good place to store our lawn mower, garden tools, and other things out of our crowded garage. Building this shed was a needed diversion from my pastoral responsibilities.

One winter day before Christmas I looked out the living room window and was shocked and excited to see four deer walking across our front lawn. Occasionally deer were killed on the B-W Parkway just a mile from our house.

Need for a Permanent Facility

For a couple years we were looking to purchase a building we could convert into a church facility. We resisted building but we finally decided this was what we needed to do. A six-acre plot, which had no sign on it, was located in Lanham. Bishop Lew told me to stop and see if the owner might be willing to sell. I stopped on Friday. When the owner answered I told him why I stopped. He said, "This is interesting because I have two contracts on my table. I'll likely accept one on Monday." We talked. Using his phone, I called Lew. I then asked the owner if he would give us a couple days to think it over. We came back and offered the full price he was asking and the land became ours. Another miracle!

Fund-Raising Banquet

To help raise funds for our new building we had a banquet. People were encouraged to give and make pledges. After the meeting there was a commotion in the poorly-lit parking lot. The police with their flashing lights came. One of the families who had come to church were recently separated. The problem arose, who gets to keep their son. After a rather lengthy passionate plea from the mother, they came to a civil agreement. We prayed. I prayed this would not hit the newspapers. Our prayers were answered. It's good to report after a few years the couple is back together again.

It took three years to find a property and it took us another three years to obtain permits and to build. We built a 26,000-square foot facility, which included an auditorium seating 375 people plus Sunday school rooms and a gymnasium. After nine years at Capitol College, we moved into our building in June 2003 at 10411 Greenbelt Rd., Lanham, MD 20706.

This Is God's Work

As people came up the walk toward our building some entered and said to me, "What is it about this place? I felt God's love before we entered the building." Tears came to my eyes as I rejoiced in what God was doing. This thrilled Helen as God was answering her prayers for God's love to be felt when people entered the property. Coffee and snacks were available for everyone both before and after the service.

One of the first Sundays a new woman entered and took the programs (bulletins) from my hand and said, "Here, I'll do that." Her assertiveness surprised me. She became a regular attender, one of my best friends and supporters.

An Exciting Funeral

When a Guyana lady died there were approximately one hundred people present at the funeral home in D.C. The undertaker told me to keep the funeral to one hour because he had several funerals lined up. Keeping a funeral to one hour in Guyanese culture was difficult because everyone has to speak. When I stood up to begin the service a woman stood and shouted, "She's a witch! She is going straight to hell!" The family of this woman got her quieted for the moment but during the service they had to continually work to keep her from speaking out. My message was quite short as many people shared stories about the deceased.

At the grave after I gave the benediction this woman started to sing "Silent Night, Holy Night." The audience joined her. Since the verse ended in "Sleep in heavenly peace," it seemed to fit after all even though it was a hot July afternoon. After the coffin was lowered it was the custom for people to throw dirt on the coffin. Somehow a large clump of dirt hit the coffin. Everyone jumped at the loud bang it made. I was glad to go home for a little peace and quiet.

A Zealous Witness

Joe sold security systems to homeowners. He rang the doorbell or knocked. When someone answered if he heard or saw a dog he would say, "Is your dog saved yet?" Different times I felt embarrassed with his direct approach. Joe died suddenly at age 63 when he had a heart attack while driving. Somehow, he got the car to the side of the road before he died. When I had his funeral people seemed to come from far and near. One person flew here from out of state to share how Joe had led him to Christ. Many others shared as well. Most of us would not appreciate Joe's straightforward approach to sharing Jesus but God used Joe to bring many to our Lord. His approach may not have been the best but he introduced more people to Jesus than those who never get around to sharing their faith.

Too often we are like Tom, a golfer. Tom invited Sam to go golfing Sunday morning. Sam said, "Sunday I'm in church." Tom said, "Give up that nonsense. You know you don't believe it." Sam replied, "What do you mean?" "I can prove you don't believe that Bible stuff," Tom replied. "I worked with you every day for twenty years. The Bible says that I'm headed for hell but you were never concerned enough to urge me to consider changing my life." Ask yourself: "Am I like Sam?"

As the late veteran missionary Don Jacobs wrote, "Most Christians need to learn to 'practice what we preach.' We Mennonites need to 'preach what we practice.'" After all, what does it matter one hundred years from now if people's stomachs are full, live in good health and have a beautiful home if they do not know Jesus. Jesus said, "Whoever believes in the Son has eternal life, but whoever rejects the Son will not see life, but God's wrath remains on them." (John 3:36).

Black Funerals

I was privileged to conduct several funerals for those of black races. These services are much more celebrative than I was used to. The funeral service focus is on heaven and the great future that awaits those who desire to meet Jesus. Perhaps we could learn from them how better to grieve as we focus on things above with Jesus and our friends in heaven. Paul reminds us: "Set your minds on things above, not on earthly things. For you died, and your life is now hidden with Christ in God." (Colossians 3:2-3).

The Zell family started to come to church. The wife had three children all to another man who left her years ago. She discovered that he was going to come and take the children by force from her. She notified the police. On an afternoon when she believed he was coming she asked me to watch the house from my car so I could be a witness. Thankfully he never showed. God's wisdom and protection are constantly needed especially when you are working with broken relationships.

Need for Assistant Pastor

Since Chet left for South American ministry, we needed an assistant pastor. Noah Kaye, a bright young man with Assemblies of God background attended Lanham Christian School. He came to Capital Christian when we were meeting at the college. I had Noah preach his first sermon at age 16. After graduation he went to Valley Forge Christian College in Phoenixville, Pennsylvania, an Assemblies of God college. During college breaks he attended CCF. Bishop Lew and I went to Phoenixville and encouraged him to consider working with me as assistant pastor when he graduated. His leadership abilities and preaching skills were well accepted by the congregation. We worked together as the congregation continued to grow.

33 Nationalities

There were twenty nationalities represented in our congregation. Each spring we had an International Sunday when everyone was encouraged to bring food representing their nation. We had people stand who were not native to the United States. One year people from thirty-three nations were present. Two little children came to the front many Sundays and danced as we sang and worshipped. One man who often came late entered and knelt in prayer before he joined in the worship.

This mix of people was a foretaste of heaven. The Apostle John describes heaven as seeing "A great multitude that no one could count from every nation, tribe, people, and language standing before the throne and before the Lamb." (Revelation 7:9). Can you imagine the excitement and joy awaiting us who know Jesus?

Ready to Retire

I was age 68 and Noah was anxious to become lead pastor. The transition went smoothly. In November I announced to the congregation that Helen and I would be terminating and moving to Pennsylvania in May 2006.

Pastor Noah and I went to the pastors' retreat at Eastern Mennonite Seminary. Noah had arranged to meet Nelson Okanya who was open to meeting with us to consider serving on the staff at CCF. He joined us a few months before Helen and I moved to Pennsylvania.

In the eight months before we left there were baptisms every month. Most of those who were baptized were adults except the one month there were two youth. Attendance was over 400. Paul said that the Philippian Church was his joy and crown. CCF was my joy and crown (Philippians 4:1). The first week of May 2006 several men helped us load the U-Haul and we headed for Manheim, Pennsylvania.

When the date came to close on our house in Laurel, our house in Manheim, Lancaster County, Pa., was not ready. God opened the door for Helen and me to live at Dr. Clarence and Helen Rutt's in Salunga for five weeks. A section of their home was designed to provide housing for missionaries. Five weeks later we moved to Brookshire, a community designed for persons age 55 and older in Manheim.

We looked forward to moving here since Lancaster Conference had a Monday evening prayer meeting at the Conference office. We were thrilled with the prayer and fellowship but disappointed that the numbers were small, usually about a dozen or fifteen. Our churches will not reach community people unless we have a passion to pray. A year later I called together Christians with a passion to share Jesus. Monthly we spent time in prayer, encouraging one another as we shared our joys and struggles in witnessing for Jesus.

Helen's Parents

Helen's father, Chester Steffy, died on October 4, 2002. Several people expressed how they appreciated his carpenter skills. He was a life-time member of EMM, serving on the Executive Committee. Through Mennonite Disaster Service he helped rebuild homes in Honduras, British Honduras, Yugoslavia and Guatemala.

Four years later Helen's mother's health was rapidly declining. Helen was anticipating being with her mother but she was greatly disappointed when she died the 24th of February 2006 just weeks before we moved to Brookshire, a retirement community near Manheim. Our three children all shared words of deep appreciation for Elizabeth at her funeral. Unfortunately, Helen was in severe pain and was hospitalized the night before the funeral. Her parents are buried at Habacker Mennonite Church Cemetery.

BISHOP

2006-2009

I wasn't finished serving CCF yet. Bishop Good was past retirement age for bishops recommended by Lancaster Conference. I agreed to serve as interim bishop for a two-year period. Many Sundays I traveled 200 miles or more round trip to meet with the congregations in the Baltimore-Washington District of Lancaster Mennonite Conference. This, along with my 48 years of pastoring, was excellent preparation for my church consultation ministry, which was soon to begin.

One pastor would not follow the advice from his elders on how he spent his time. He ignored their request. He believed he could possess the church building but it was deeded so the elders were the owners. When he was shown the papers from the lawyer, he finally left with a few of the members. I walked with the remaining group. Healing was slow but they are moving forward and growing.

Meeting monthly with the bishops at the Conference Office was usually very uplifting. There were a few times as in Acts 15 we were in sharp dispute but God's Spirit got us through. One practice that was most helpful was "Dwelling in the Word." We would take the same Scriptural passage each month for several months, as Luke 10 where Jesus sent out the 72 disciples or Acts 2, which describes the birthday of the church, and asked what God is saying to those when it was written and then ask how it speaks to us. It is amazing how the same passage brings truth that is relevant to the particular issues we face today.

One main concern was to find dedicated pastors. We prayed for the Lord to raise up young men and women for pastoral leadership. Jesus said, "Pray for the Lord of the harvest to send out laborers into His harvest." (Matthew 9:38).

ALASKA CRUISE—JULY 23-30, GIFT FROM CCF

2006

As a going-away gift CCF blessed us with a cruise. After moving and getting things unpacked and in place, we chose an Alaska Cruise, on the Holland American Line. What an adventure! We were assigned a room on the lower level of the ship. The second night Helen woke me up yelling, "Get up! There's water on our floor and it's rising higher." I jumped out of bed, hurriedly dressed and tossed our possessions in the suitcases, then waded through the rising waters as we headed upstairs. Unlike the *Titanic* it was only a water pipe that burst. Waiting in the hall with our possessions we were finally assigned another room.

Helen enjoyed walking around the long deck. I saw whales in the distance. I had quality time reading much of Oswald Chamber's devotional, *My Upmost for His Highest*. If you want to walk closer to Jesus read this book. It's read by more people than any other devotional book.

On our off-shore excursions we were amazed by the beautiful flowers on the hillsides. One of the highlights, especially for Helen, was the 60-minute flight on a six-passenger float-equipped bush plane through the Tongass National Forest. We enjoyed the personal narration from our bush pilot as we flew over the wonders of nature. We saw majestic fjords, waterfalls, lakes and groups of hardy mountain goats. The smooth landing on the lake was a new experience.

On another excursion we could see in the distance the 20,000+ foot-high Mount McKinley, the highest elevation in North America. Land or sea it was a special time we enjoyed together.

AUTHOR

2007

Several persons were encouraging me to write the story of Capital Christian Fellowship. English classes were difficult for me. I never thought I would be a writer. I wrote for a year. Herald Press looked over what I had written. They offered to edit and publish the book. The editor did an excellent job and after another year it was published in 2009 under the title: *Now Go Forward: Reaching Out to Grow Your Congregation.* They printed 2,400 copies. I had the privilege of selling many of them to fellow pastors and churches. It is presently out of print except for e-books.

I lived my life with a passion to share Jesus. I felt I needed to pass this passion on to others. One way to do that was to write a devotional book. I entitled it: *Living With Godly Passion: 366 Devotionals for Those with a Passion to Share Jesus* published in 2010. The next year, I wrote a shorter devotional, *Power Scriptures for Successful Living, 366 Timely Devotionals* published in 2011. Helen was most helpful in reading, checking sentence structure and spelling, etc.

CHURCH CONSULTATION

2006-2010

Before we moved from CCF I was in dialogue with EMM and Lancaster Conference concerning the possibility of serving as a church consultant. I had 50 years of pastoring both rural and urban growing congregations, traditional Mennonite congregations as well as those on the cutting edge. Above all I had a passion to see churches grow and plant churches. Many persons from Lancaster Mennonite Conference and EMM had been to Capital Christian Fellowship and observed God's moving among us. Others had read my 300-page book, *Now Go Forward: Reaching Out to Grow your Congregation.* This helped to open the door for consultation ministry.

EMM required all missionaries to have a missionary support team. We set a goal of $1700 a month for my part-time salary. I would be responsible to Lancaster Conference but supported through EMM. I asked three persons from CCF and three in Lancaster County to be my missionary support team. Lewis Good from CCF chaired the team. We met monthly mostly via teleconferencing. When I spoke at different churches, I took my books with me. In this way I was able to raise several hundred dollars each month from the sale of my books and from honorariums. Individual contributions made up the remainder of my salary.

All missionaries with EMM were required to participate in their three-week Missionary Training Institute. At age 71, I sat among many who were entering the mission field for the first time. It was a joy to hear their call to leave family, friends, house and land to build God's Kingdom in the far corners of the world. Jesus said, "No one who has left home, or brothers or sisters or mother or father or children or fields for me and the gospel will fail to receive a hundred times as much in this present age... along with persecutions – and in the age to come eternal life." (Mark 10:29-30).

I designed a pamphlet to distribute to pastors. At our annual conference the leadership placed this pamphlet on each table of delegates. I was invited to meet with a number of church leadership teams and frequently asked to speak at Sunday morning services. A number of bishops invited the leadership teams of their churches for Saturday morning and afternoon presentations.

I used power points conveying the necessity of reaching out to our communities, presenting many possible approaches I had used. Usually, the interchange was vigorous. All in all, I ministered in about 70 congregations in ten states and eight different conferences. When I walked into one church I asked an older lady if she came here all her life. Her response was, "No, I didn't die yet!" Her humor was refreshing.

I needed an interpreter for a large Spanish church in North Carolina as I ministered there from Friday through Sunday. Pastors in Franklin Mennonite Conference were especially receptive as they invited me to return for follow-up consultations. After being at Clinton Frame Church in Indiana I returned on a weekend to equip their evangelists and those who had a passion to share Jesus. Invitations slacked off after three years. Furthermore, I didn't enjoy asking people to contribute to my missionary support team; I was ready for a change.

Slow to Adapt New Wineskins

Churches are very slow to change, to adapt new wineskins (Matthew 9:16-17). Many members as well as pastors shake their head in agreement as to what needs to be done but find it out of the question to bring about systemic changes that will cause the church to line up with Jesus' radical demands. For example, everyone agrees we need to obey Jesus' Great Commission but few put it into action or even sincerely pray about how they are to implement it. On a smaller scale, visitors to a church with a cracked window pane will notice while members tend to think it is not important. It's often the little things we overlook that catch the attention of visitors giving them a negative feeling.

Vision Is Primary

Lack of vision is my main concern for most established churches. Without a vision we perish (Proverbs 28:18 KJV). Paul says we are to forget our past mistakes and focus or strain forward to what lies ahead (Philippians 3:13). Closely related to lack of vision is lack of prayer. Too often in leadership meetings the agenda seems to be, we'll offer a token prayer and then get on with the business. The main business is prayer. After we pray then we can be led by the Holy Spirit to discern our direction.

"The discipline of prayer is the intentional, concentrated and regular effort to create space for God. Everything and everyone around us wants to fill up every bit of space in our lives and so make us not only occupied people but preoccupied people as well. When we learn to regard prayer as the highest part of the work entrusted to us, the root and strength of all other work, we shall see that there is nothing that we need to practice as the art of praying aright." (Andrew Murry in *With Christ in the School of Prayer*, pp. 8 & 72.)

Eastern Mennonite Seminary asked me to teach an extension course on their Lancaster Campus. I enjoyed the challenge of teaching "Reaching Your Community for Christ," helping these fifteen pastors and church leaders structure their congregation to impact their community for Christ.

I was the resource speaker for the Retired Pastors' Retreat at Black Rock Camp. Many had the attitude, "I had my turn, let the younger men and women pick up the mantel." I challenged the fifty-some participants to not rest on their laurels but claim David's promise in Psalm 92:14, "The righteous will still bear fruit in old age, they will stay fresh and green, proclaiming, the Lord is upright; he is my Rock." "Never be lacking in zeal, but keep your spiritual zeal, serving the Lord." (Romans 12:11).

About once a summer I went to a professional or semi-professional ball game. Nearly every time I see a crowd, whether in person or on TV, I think of Jesus. When He saw a crowd, He had compassion on them because He saw the people as sheep without a shepherd. When you see a crowd do you see them as Jesus did: Sheep without a Shepherd? Jesus then instructs us to pray for the Lord to send out workers into the harvest (Matthew 9:36-38). I ask myself, "I wonder how many of these people will be in heaven?" Jesus said, "The road leading to destruction is broad and many take that road but the way to life is narrow and only a few choose that road." (Matthew 7:13-14). The fields are ready for harvest (John 4:35). Prayers, prayed at the ball field will make a difference for eternity.

Here Comes Inspiration

Helen enjoys using her God-given gift of encouragement. In order to continue using her hand, she required extensive therapy following surgery on her hand. In the therapy room, she with others struggled to do the painful exercises necessary for healing. She encouraged others. One day as she entered the room, one of the fellows called out, "Here comes inspiration!" "Say only what is helpful in building others up according to their needs, that it may benefit those who listen." (Ephesians 4:29).

Great-Grandchildren

"Children are an inheritance from the Lord." (Psalm 127:3). Each one is special. Noel became a grandmother and we became great-grandparents.

April 20, 2010, Isaiah James Miller
was born to Dustin and Amy.

July 25, 2014, Adilyn Noel
was born to Dustin and Kylee.

July 23, 2016, Brody Allen
was born to Brett and Katie Martz.

January 24, 2022 Baylor Andrew
was born to Brett and Katie Martz.

March 2, 2022, Levi David
was born to Micah and Audrey Engle-Eshleman.

We believe each child is uniquely gifted by God. We pray they use their gifts to bring honor and glory to God passing their faith on from one generation to the next.

THE CALL FROM OHIO

2011-2019

Our son Chet, while serving with MCC in Columbia, South America, had a clear word from the Lord that he should begin a church in Ohio. That same week he received a letter from the ministers in Holmes County, Ohio, asking him to come and plant a church in Dover, Ohio, east of Holmes County and twenty miles south of Canton. What a clear confirmation of his call! He and his family moved to Dover.

Chet kept calling Helen and me, telling us we are needed to help plant the church in Dover. After a long phone conversation in December of 2010, we knew God was calling us to move to Dover even though when we moved to Brookshire in Manheim, we thought this was our retirement home. We were finally settled. Furthermore, I was age 75. Back to Ohio again!

We looked at several houses that Chet had picked out for us to consider. We knew when we walked into a small ranch house on North Crater Avenue that this open floor plan was the one for us. However, from the first step inside the door there was an obvious problem. Helen is allergic to cigarette smoke. The woman who had lived there was a chain-smoker. We removed all the carpets with their cigarette burns, tried in vain to remove cigarette stains from the rim of the bath tub and washbowl, painted all the walls and ceiling with "Killes," and washed the smoke-stained windows as the cigarette tar dripped its brown juice into our buckets. By the time Helen arrived a few days later all was clean—no odors.

We enjoyed watching the neighbor children playing in their backyard. Helen didn't enjoy being kept awake until two or three in the morning with their occasional beer parties. The high school boys across the street tested our patience practicing on the drums. From the kitchen window we could see in the not-to-distance a beautiful mansion where the man committed suicide. Apparently, his riches did not satisfy.

For the majority of our neighbors church was a place to go if it was convenient. Others slept in or went to a cabin on the beach. On one occasion the ten-year-old neighbor boy said to me, "Sunday I am going to be baptized. You're a pastor, what does baptism mean?"

It had been 20 years since we moved from Elyria, Ohio. I was hoping I could do church consulting work. Several opportunities came but not to the extent I had hoped. Many pastors I worked with twenty years ago had changed positions. The new leadership did not know me.

Chet and Holly had pulled together a church of about fifty persons from all walks of life. There was a doctor, nurse, and two small business owners with the majority of people coming from an Appalachian background.

The group chose the name LifeBridge Community Fellowship. To begin they met in Chet and Holly's home. Outgrowing their living room, they met in a hotel lobby. On the square of Dover stood a 100-year-old building. It was originally a beautiful Methodist Church with its large stained-glass windows. After the Methodist Church moved out of the building it became the home of the Salvation Army for thirty or more years. LifeBridge purchased this stately building and began making numerous repairs and renovations.

I was "errand boy" for Chet: Getting the church mail, answering the phone, and meeting persons who came when Chet was not in his study. I led the Sunday prayer time, which met before church. We passed out flyers inviting our neighbors to church. Since our church building was on the square it was not unusual for people to stop and ask for rent or gas money. A few times each year I had a weekly Scriptural meditation on the local radio station.

Making Disciples

From a child I had wanted to have a radio ministry. The opportunity came in 2014 when World Harvest Radio in Indiana had an opening for a three- to five-minute daily program on their shortwave stations reaching Europe, Asia, Africa and South America. This ministry would cost us more than a $1000 a month. I named the program "Making Disciples." After the first year Helen joined me as we used a dialogue format in delivering the messages. After two and one-half years due to the time spent in preparing and presenting the messages and the difficulty of raising the funds, we felt led to terminate these programs.

One of my favorite promises in the Bible is Isaiah 55:11, "My word which goes out from my mouth will accomplish what I desire and achieve the purpose for which I sent it." I pray every day that God's Word going out over the airways around the world will reach even the two billion people who have never heard the Good News and that tens of thousands will experience new life in Jesus. It will not return void.

Buzzing with Life

LifeBridge is an active church. Most of the Sunday morning attenders came to the Sunday afternoon soccer games at Dover's beautiful park. Women with their babies came and sat on the sidelines. Sunday evening carry-in meals at various homes followed by games were frequently enjoyed by most everyone.

One unique ministry of LifeBridge was their Sunday noon meals each week. Two families rotated with others to provide the weekly meals. One Sunday a month everyone was asked to bring food to share. This time of fellowship contributed much to the healthy life of the church. Since we didn't have a gymnasium, in the winter we rented the Christian Missionary Alliance gym just a block up the street to play games.

LifeBridge delivered food from the community food bank to needy families. The Jay Yoder family worked tirelessly teaching their children the joy of sharing to those in need. Others also, including myself, gave time to help deliver food.

Another ministry of LifeBridge was helping people move. Several persons had pickup trucks. The women brought food. People greatly appreciated this ministry. All six churches I pastored helped people move.

Living Room Prayer Group

Helen and I lead a bi-weekly prayer group in our living room. I led a weekly men's Bible study; with the majority of the men having spent time in prison. One man, who had been imprisoned for a couple years, kept growing in his walk with the Lord. He was able to get a job. Today he is teaching his own group.

Another man in our Bible study group had been promiscuous. Life went downhill until he finally ended up sleeping in the street and spent time in prison. After divorcing his wife, she married another man, which fueled his anger. His only child, a daughter, refused to see him. Alcohol became an escape but only for a few hours. The Salvation Army ministered to him. He struggled for years to put off his old habits. With the encouragement and prayers of our group he is a new man in Christ. He loves his Bible and shares what he learns with everyone who will listen.

Ken, a homeless man, often slept on the cement slab at the entrance of our church. We tried to communicate but he was tight-lipped about his life and trusted no one. He refused to go to a shelter unless it was extremely cold. We provided food, showed love and tried to get him to come into the church building especially when we had meals in the church basement. He pulled a lawnmower with him, which he used to mow lawns. Pastor Chet gave him $5 to mow the tiny lawn on the side of the church building. We prayed he would open his heart to God's healing love.

I called new movers just as I had at CCF. After several calls and visits Ron came to church. He was an unwanted child. His mother kicked him out of the house and told him never to return. He had been married seven times. His present wife had been abused as a child and was raised with many non-Christian superstitions, which were deeply embedded in her mind. Helen and I met with them for many months. Both accepted Christ and are growing in their walk with the Lord. How precious it is to experience the life-transformation of salvation. They are transformed by the renewing of their minds (Romans 12:2).

Attempted Church Plant in Strasburg

Chet recruited a young couple with children to church plant. He had pastored a church in Pennsylvania. We helped them move and gave them three families from LifeBridge. The work grew slowly. Some of the larger Mennonite Churches in Holmes County sent persons to help provide a core group. I and a couple from Dover helped by attending there on Sunday evenings. It seems most everything Chet suggested he did not follow. A neighbor church of another denomination with a more liberal theology needed a pastor. He applied and was accepted where he continues today.

Writing

In my spare time I kept writing. *Soaring on Eagle's Wings: When the Supernatural Becomes Natural, 366 Devotional Readings* and *Let the Bible Speak for Itself: 101 Essays; Questions We All Ask* were both published in 2018.

I was anxious to get my books into the hands of both believers and especially non-believers. There are two large flea markets a few miles east of Dover, one in Sugarcreek and one in Berlin. Busloads come from several states, especially from Kentucky. God opened the door for me to sell my books there. Helen's ministry as always, was at home, praying for me and the clients. I estimate I sold close to two thousand books there. Even though I came home very tired I enjoyed talking with people about my books and the joy of serving Jesus. An adjudicating question I received was, "What version do you use." I knew that meant they were not interested because for most of them anything other than King James was out.

Men's 6:30 A.M. Group

The weekly men's group met in a restaurant every Wednesday. It was the most disciplined group of my life. Often in the winter months the thermometer reading was zero at 6:30 a.m. when we met. The group continues to this day. It's been effective because, first, the Bible was our textbook. No matter how good other books are the Bible must be our main focus. Secondly, Chet, our leader was transparent and honest before God and us men. This opened the door for us to share deeply. A third reason it was effective was that it consisted of men from various backgrounds, denominations and even seekers who had no church home. This type of disciplined small group is the key to making disciples and extending God's Kingdom. Can we find Christians today who will discipline themselves to meet regularly and challenge each other in their walk with Christ even though it may be inconvenient?

John was a skilled carpenter. He spent several years in prison where he read and memorized Scripture. He amazed us with his knowledge of Scripture. Everyone loved John's gentle spirit. But John would never reveal his past life. Someone said, "We are as sick as our secrets." Jesus said, "It's the truth that sets us free." (John 8:31). John shocked us when he apparently took too many pills committing suicide. God forgives us of our sins if we confess them (I John 1:9). However, we often need to confess our sins to each other to experience healing. James 5:16 NLT, "Confess your sins to each other and pray for each other so that you may be healed. The earnest pray for a righteous person has great power and wonderful results." "Whoever conceals their sins does not prosper, but the one who confesses and renounces them finds mercy." (Proverbs 28:13).

Thrift Store

LifeBridge began a thrift store in our church basement. The church was blessed as people, especially those on the fringes got involved in sorting clothes, clearing and filling racks. The thrift store is especially helpful to the many Guatemalan families in our community.

Kathy, our thrift store manager, related well to women who were in rehab for various addictions. She'd bring some of these women to help with the store and to relate to the other workers. This was an effective ministry and continues to this day in a more intense way with a home, "Beneath the Shade," proving a safe place for women. It was normal for a few persons to come to Sunday worship, leave when the children were dismissed for their class and smoke their cigarettes outside and then return to church for the sermon.

We needed more room for our growing congregation. Some Sundays we had an attendance of 150. An addition was added onto our church building in 2018 for our growing attendance and the thrift store.

Jerry, a Christian businessman with several employees asked if I would meet with him to be his mentor. We met every two weeks for more than a year. We talked about how his life could be more integrated with Christ. Jerry got up early in the morning and watched the news for thirty minutes.

I kept praying and urging Jerry to study God's Word. The only book that spoke to him was Proverbs. He just could not get himself to love God's Word. His mind was dominated by his business and by the news. His dad was a Bible teacher but did some things that really turned him off. Until he fully forgives his father's inconsistencies, he will never know the joy of reading and studying God's Word. "Let the Word of God dwell in you richly." (Colossians 3:16). "All Scripture is God-breathed and is useful for teaching, rebuking, correcting and training in righteousness, so that the servant of God may be thoroughly equipped for every good work." (II Timothy 3:16-17).

50th Wedding Anniversary

For four days our family had a delightful time at Holly's parents, Abe and Mary Miller's cabin in Holmes County to celebrate our 50th wedding anniversary. We hiked, played games, swam and fished in the lake. Morning and evening group devotionals were enriching. We talked about Colossians 1:17 in which Jesus is the key that holds all things together. Laminin is the protein molecule in our bodies that holds things together. The fascinating thing about laminin is that it is shaped in the form of a cross. Amazing!

Health Issues

Chet experienced major health issues related to E-Coli, which left him weak for months. At the same time, he believed God was calling him to transition to plant another church. This meant Helen and I were faced with a major decision. We both had health issues. I had prostate cancer. Not long after that my heart had to be shocked to get it into rhythm. Helen lives with five incurable conditions: Osteoarthropathy, Peripheral Neuropathy in her hands and feet, Waldenström's Macroglobulinemia (a rare blood cancer), Macular Degeneration and Erosive Oral Lichen Planus.

Helen says, "Each day I choose to rejoice in the Lord regardless of my pain level. Attitude is extremely important to me. I encourage myself with God's Word. I'm humbly blessed by people who pray for me. I ask God to especially bless them as prayer is a most precious gift."

With Chet's family moving away should we stay here? For many years I had promised Helen we would return to Lancaster County, Pennsylvania, to be with our families when we retire. We thought when we moved to Brookshire in 2006 that would be our last move. This was now 13 years later! I am blessed with a patient and wonderful wife.

LANDIS HOMES RETIREMENT COMMUNITY

2019....

We applied to Landis Homes Retirement Community near Lititz, Pennsylvania. Faith and her husband John Nissley lived there for the past ten years. We visited them many times. Both our parents lived there before they died. Helen's father, Chester Steffy, was foreman for the building crew—building some of the earlier buildings. Persons usually had to wait more than a year before there was room to move here. God miraculously opened the door to move almost as soon as we could sell our house, which sold to a neighbor within days.

With the help of our friends at LifeBridge we packed the U-Haul and moved to Landis Homes on August 1, 2019. Wil and Barbara Good, who were a great help to us at CCF, had moved to Landis Homes. She arranged for some persons to bring in food and to help unload the truck. We downsized to a 639 sq. ft. apartment. We are thankful for an extra storage unit that Barbara arranged for us to use. Helen had moved 21 times in her life. Since our marriage we moved 15 times. We hope this will be our final move before our move to our home in heaven.

Opportunities for Ministry

Soon after I arrived at Landis Homes, I bumped into Ginny Hartman, a member of the pastoral staff. She remembered me as a pastor when we lived in Lima. I had had a series of renewal meetings and had preached several times at Pike Mennonite Church, which was her home church in Elida. She asked if I would be willing to have morning devotions on our

TV station. God opened the door almost upon our arrival. Helen joined me for dialogue messages until she resigned for health reasons. I have the privilege of presenting these devotional messages twice each month. Occasionally I teach the Sunday School lesson over the TV. When people thank me, I think of Corrie ten Boon's response: She offers the thanks as a bouquet to God in praise (Hebrews 13:15). Helen and I enjoy the many activities and programs offered to the approximately 950 residents.

Helen walks the halls here at Landis Homes encouraging people with her joyful greetings. Both workers and residents see her as a person of inspiration. Her typical answer to those who ask, "How are you?" is, "I'm praising the Lord!" At times people tell her God's light shines through her eyes.

Helen's life of praising God grows out of her close communion with God. She spends hours in His presence, bathing her soul and spirit in His love. Zephaniah 3:17 is one of her favorite verses: "The Lord your God is among you; He is mighty to save. He will rejoice over you with gladness; He will quiet you with His love; He will rejoice over you with singing." Living in pain drives her closer to Jesus day by day. Isaiah 48:10 NLT, God says, "I have refined you in the furnace of suffering."

Nearly everyone, workers and residents are very congenial. Occasionally I bump into a man or two who are always complaining. No matter how I try to point out God's goodness in the situation they find a rebuttal. They are not happy people! Paul writes that we are to do all things without complaining or arguing (Philippians 2:14-15).

60th Wedding Anniversary

We enjoyed a quiet day together, feeling so blessed for the sixty years we had together. Living in a retirement home there are several deaths every week. Heaven seems closer than ever. How blessed we are to have God's peaceful assurance of spending eternity with Him. God's mercies are new every day and great is His faithfulness (Lamentation 3:23). We thank God for His daily care and bountiful provision.

Faith's Death and Scattered Family

Faith died rather suddenly, October 15, 2021, with lung cancer. Jesus said, "I am the resurrection and the life. The one who believes in me will live, even though they die; and whoever lives by believing in me will never die." (John 11:25-26). Helen and I miss her daily visits. Living here twelve years she had a multitude of friends. She visited John daily in the dementia unit as the Covid-19 pandemic permitted. At her funeral Chet gave the message. Scott and his wife, Joy, shared words of appreciation. We were thankful that John, her husband, could attend her funeral.

Our children are scattered: Scott in Chicago, Illinois; Chet in Goshen, Indiana; and Noel in Bristle, Indiana. It's always a delight to hear their voice via phone. Our usual pattern is to talk weekly catching up on each grandchild. As the Apostle John writes, "I have no greater joy than to hear that my children are walking in the truth." (III John 4). Helen and I pray daily for each member of our family.

Church Family

Through my church consulting work I learned to know a few persons at Landis Valley Christian Fellowship just two miles from Landis Homes. Barbara Good had arranged for them to help us move into our apartment here. Their loving help also helped us to choose Landis Valley as our church. We deeply appreciate the dedicated leaders there and the children's involvement in the worship services. Because of the coronavirus pandemic I enjoy the Thursday evening zoom prayer and Bible study time.

Writing: My New Passion

Before we moved from Dover I had written, *Fierce Love: Balancing God's Love and Justice.* After we moved, I finished *God's Hall of Faith Speaks Today: Hebrews 11.* A verse that continually amazed me, which I couldn't get out of my mind was Jesus' words concerning John the Baptist: "Truly I tell you, among those born of women there has not risen anyone greater than John the Baptist; yet whoever is least in the kingdom of heaven is greater than he." (Matthew 11:11). How could I be greater than all the Old Testament men and women of God? This led to my writing of *75 Scriptures that Will Amaze You: Living on a Higher Plane.* It has proved to be my best seller. People return to tell me how this book has encouraged them.

There are two large farmer's markets here: one in Landisville called Roots and the other in Ephrata named Green Dragon. Both are open one day a week. I recently discovered there is a monthly flea market in Leola. Since it is inside, I can go in winter. The Sunday before my autobiography went to press, I asked my Christian Education class to pray that I would be able to get my books in the hands of persons who were not committed Christians. The teacher and the pastor laid their hands on me as we prayed. Monday morning, I received a call from a gentleman who wanted to purchase 15 books for the youth of his church and for friends. In the five years I had been going to farmer's markets I had not received a call like this. Tuesday, I went to Roots Market and sold 22 books, the most I had sold in one day.

The next time I returned to Roots, Missionaries to Haiti purchased a book their daughter, who was born in Haiti, will use to teach the youth in their growing church.

After coming home from Green Dragon on Friday, July 15, 2022, I received this email. "I bought your book today: *75 Scriptures That Will Amaze You.* I have to tell you it is truly amazing. I recently have been wanting to learn and study God's Word more and this is exactly what I was looking for. Already your book has changed the way I think and look at God. I just want to say 'Thank you.' I feel this was truly the answer to my prayer."

Joel says, "I will pour out my Spirit on all people. Your sons and daughters will prophesy, your old men will dream dreams, and your young men will see visions. Even on my servants, both men and women, I will pour out my Spirit." (Joel 2:28-29). For weeks I have been having nightly dreams of God's Spirit pulling together people from all walks of life worshipping God.

I cry with Habakkuk; how long must I see daily violence and injustice on the TV news? Habakkuk is told to write down the revelation for everyone to read. "The revelation awaits an appointed time; it speaks of the end and will not prove false. Though it will linger, wait for it; it will certainly come and will not delay." (2:2-3). "The earth will be filled with the knowledge of the glory of the Lord as the waters cover the sea." (2:14). Though there will be very difficult times ahead when your people will experience famine – crops and orchards will wither, and there is no paycheck, yet you are to rejoice in the

Lord. (3:17-19). God is saying, "Dave, wait patiently and rejoice in the Lord."

In 1999, God gave me a prayer that I have prayed over and over: "I pray that tens of thousands may come to know the Lord and millions be encouraged, even that is too small." I believe God will answer that prayer long after I am not here. As Helen and I pray, my books are being carried to many countries of the world, via missionaries taking the books with them.

As this book goes to press I am working on what I except will be my final book: *God Speaks to His Church: Revelation 2 and 3.*

Deeds Are Not Forgotten

While selling my books at Roots a gentleman came and asked if I knew who he was. I didn't remember him. He said, "When I started farming, your Dad brought me a load of hay because I was having a difficult time. Your Dad would not take any remuneration." Dad died thirty years ago. God says, "Blessed are the dead who die in the Lord from now on. They will rest from their labor, for their deeds will follow them." (Revelation 14:13). How blessed I am to know that my dad who worked so hard all this life is resting from his labor and his deeds still speak today!

Not long after we arrived here Helen teamed up with me to give dialogue devotionals over the TV. These were especially appreciated. We decided to put them into a book entitled: *50 Scriptural Meditations,* which was published in 2021. Sometimes when I am selling my books people ask if I have any large print books. I had my best seller, *75 Scriptures That Will Amaze You* put in large print in 2021.

World Prayer

I felt the burden to pray for world needs and approached Donna Mack Shenk the Director of Pastoral Services if we could begin a world prayer time. She said to contact Richard Weaver who also expressed interest. A weekly group of about a dozen persons met in East Bethany Chapel until the Covid-19 Pandemic came. We transitioned to a 15-minute weekly TV program: "World Prayer." Janet Breneman joined us in leading the program. After a year both Richard and I had health issues. We were unable to find others to lead and decided to discontinue the program.

Staying Physically Fit

At age 85 life can become quite sedentary as I sit to read, to work on my computer and watch TV. I live with a pacemaker, a cochlear hearing device and a permanent catheter. The emergency room has been all too familiar because of repeated kidney stones. Paul says, "We do not lose heart. Though outwardly we are wasting away, yet inwardly we are being renewed day by day." (II Corinthians 4:16).

The physical therapy machines are available here but I prefer the outdoors. Spring, summer and fall I ride bike. Since I cannot comfortably lift my leg over the bar of a boy's bike, I ride Faith's 40-year-old bike.

Riding in the Leaman Woods here on campus is a challenge. It takes all my strength with my old bike to make it to the top of the grade. I stop there to rest and use the "covered bridge" as a prayer closet or sit on the bench overlooking the huge soybean fields and talk to God. Riding past the ponds I need to slow up to avoid hitting the ducks or geese and trying to miss their droppings.

I enjoy riding in the country past the Amish one-room school. I hear the children chattering in Pennsylvania Dutch as they play softball, and swing on the swings and up and down on the sea-saws. Seeing the well-kept gardens causes me to thank God for people who take pride in their work. Cows, horses, mules, and a pony perk up their ears as I ride by talking to them. I can almost touch them as they stand against the fence. Looking up I see God's majestic heavens. Frequently hot air balloons glide slowly by or an airplane slowing up as it approaches the landing strip at the Lititz Airport. God is everywhere. I feel His presence. I shout praises to Him with tongues of men and of angels (I Corinthians 13:1).

In the dead of winter when it is too cold to ride, I prefer exercising by going up and down several flights of stairs in the Crossings Building rather than go to the fitness center. Furthermore, it's not unusual to find a dish of candy on the shelf just outside the residents' doors.

The Mission Field Is Here

We never need to wonder where we are needed. Approximately nine percent of older adults in the U.S. have dementia. 61,000,000 adults or two in five age 65 and older live with a disability. Many of these persons are lonely. Many never have a friend or relative visit them. For two years I meet with a man every two weeks who has a mild form of dementia. He thanks me profusely every time. John, my brother-in-law who lives in a dementia unit also appreciates my visits. Show God's love by visiting, encouraging and helping any way you can. When we serve these people, we are serving Jesus (Matthew 25:40). "Always give yourself fully to the work of the Lord, because you know that your labor in the Lord is not in vain." (I Corinthians 15:58).

Paul commands us to "make the most of every opportunity because the days are evil." (Ephesians 5:16). I pray daily to fulfill that command. Helen and I find God amazingly answers our prayers. This results in joy and thanksgiving (v. 20).

Prayer Warrior

In my last years of pastoral ministry, from time-to-time I mentioned that perhaps our greatest temptations would come when we are physically unable to care for ourselves. I struggled with being a prayer warrior. I made the excuse as a pastor I was too busy. I prayed that my prayer life would be greatly enriched when I no longer had pastoral responsibilities. God is answering that prayer. At times I feel I'm at one with Christ experiencing the intimate relationship Paul describes in Galatians 2:20, "I have been crucified with Christ and I no longer live, but Christ lives in me. The life I now live in the body, I live by faith in the Son of God, who loved me and gave himself for me."

Since we moved here three years ago, I have daily tried to pray for many countries of the world. I often begin in the morning and pray for those primarily in North and South America, in the afternoon or evening I pray for those in Africa and Asia. It is thrilling to think that I am making a difference in these scores of countries. Often, I don't know what or how to pray but God has blessed me with the gift of praying in tongues. It's thrilling to realize that the Holy Spirit takes my stammering tongue and intercedes for me and through me to minister to the multitudes of lost and suffering people around the world (Romans 8:26 and 34).

Pray for the persecuted Christians in more than 100 countries of our world. Pray that the peace of God will transcend the pain and torture they are experiencing. Many times, as I am praying, I look out the window, it seems God sends the goldfinch darting by, the geese flying in perfect formation, the Amish horse and buggy, or special cloud formations that speak clearly of God's greatness and encourages my faith. What a tremendous privilege it is to be God's prayer warrior.

Live with Joy

In my years of pastoring, I had ministered in many retirement homes. My observation has been that few live a joyful Christian life. On different occasions, I have said that if you think you are having trials now you will likely have greater trials when you are bedfast in a retirement or nursing home. Helen and I consciously make it our daily habit to have a vital prayer life and devotional life as we pray together. We claim Jesus' promise that if we drink of Him, we will overflow with springs or rivers of living water (John 7:39). Our prayer is for His Spirit to saturate our every cell, putting a smile on our face, a spring in our step and a song in our hearts. To God be the glory! Together we follow hard after God. (Psalm 63:8 KJV).

FINAL REFLECTIONS, CONVICTIONS AND CONCERNS

These final pages reveal once again the passion of my heart.

1. God has blessed me beyond what I can convey in words. I look at my 85 years as a miracle, one miracle after another. I was a stuttering, shy kid, full of self-pity with a low self-esteem. It is only by the grace of God that He could use me to reach anyone for Christ. I have been called an apostle, a prophet, an evangelist, a pastor, a teacher and author.

In checking my emails today, I found these words from a friend: "Your devotional reading, from your book: *Living with Godly Passion,* reminded me of the days with Helen and you at Cottage City/Capital Christian Fellowship. We continue to remember how you loved on people, prayed for people, and encouraged people to do what they love and use their gifts. May we continue to follow your example and spread God's love..." I feel so unworthy when reading these words.

2. The Bible is God's eternal Word. Jesus said, "Heaven and earth will pass away but my word will never pass away." (Matthew 24:35). Again, He said, "My word is truth." (John 17:17). Say with David, "Oh, how I love your law it is my meditation all day long." (Psalm 119:97). You cannot be a disciple without loving God's Word.

Read the Bible through the lens of Jesus. God spoke through the prophets but now He has spoken through His Son, who made all things. (Hebrews 1:1-4). Jesus said five times in Matthew 5, "You have heard it said, but I say unto you." Then He explains how His interpretation superseded the Old Testament law. Whenever it seems there are different standards in the Bible always follow the New Testament. Because of the hardness of their hearts God permitted some things in the Old Testament that He did not permit in the New Testament. (Matthew 19:8).

3. Prayer is the most unutilized gift God has given us. Sincere prayer is faith in action. Without faith we cannot please God (Hebrews 11:6). With faith all things are possible (Luke 1:37). The earnest prayer of a righteous person is powerful and effective (James 5:16). Multiple times Jesus promised that we can ask anything in His name and He will do it (John 15:16). The early church devoted themselves to prayer (Acts 2:42).

I have been challenged by persons who prayed much. Paul travailed in prayer (Galatians 4:19). George Mueller spent 2-3 hours daily in the Word and in prayer. John Welsh wrote before he died that he counted the day ill-spent that he did not spend seven or eight hours in secret prayer. The unknown author in *The Kneeling Christian* writes (p.17): "Do we realize that there is nothing the devil dreads so much as prayer? His great concern is to keep us from praying. He loves to see us up to our eyes in work - provided we do not pray. He does not fear because we are eager and earnest Bible students - provided we are little in prayer. Satan laughs at our foiling, mocks at our wisdom, but trembles when we pray." This explains why consistent prayer is the most difficult activity and the most effective activity you can do. Any success I had in ministry I owe to a great extent the prayers of my wife, Helen.

God gave me a prayer twelve or more years ago, which I have prayed basically every day: "Father, You gave Your Son for me. I don't have Your passion, give me Your passion and the strength and wisdom to carry it out. Jesus, You died on the cruel cross for me. I don't have Your passion. Give me the strength and wisdom to carry my cross. Holy Spirit, You left heaven in all its splendor to come and live in my sinful heart, now being made holy by Your work. Give me Your passion, the strength and wisdom to live your life through me."

4. Our culture is on a moral downhill slide. My burden is for the church to remain pure, to be the salt and light Jesus intended it to be. We forget the primary call of the church is to proclaim the Good News. The Good News includes the mandate to feed the hungry, clothe the naked, provide for the homeless, follow justice but in

emphasizing meeting the physical needs of people we are forgetting that unless people repent, they will be lost for eternity. Today the majority who identify themselves as Christians don't believe in hell. They believe they will somehow make it to heaven without repentance. Jesus said that unless you repent you will perish (Luke 13:3-5).

Nothing has torn the church apart like the LBGTQ (lesbian, gay, bisexual and transgender) controversy. Romans 1:26-27, I Corinthians 6:10 and I Timothy 1:10 are clear that homosexuality is sin. God loves everyone and we as God's children are to love everyone. I lived beside a homosexual couple for many years and have worked with such persons. The New Testament is clear that sex outside of one man and one woman who are married is not acceptable. The world has infiltrated the Christian community where the majority of Christians claim that sex outside of marriage is acceptable. Several of our Mennonite colleges have led the way to accepting the world's standards. It's obvious why the church has lost its influence in the world.

My response when asked about the future of the Mennonite Church is that we have a great future abroad. For example, Tanzania is only one-tenth the size of the U.S. and has only one-sixth of our population. The Mennonite Church there has a goal of one million members in the coming decade, while we here are reporting stagnant growth. The people of color outnumber the Caucasians in our church and they generally speaking are conservative in their theology. This gives me great hope for our future. I'm not concerned about the name "Mennonite," I'm concerned about the purity of the church.

The Bible is clear that killing of children is murder yet many ignore this fact. The New Testament presents seventeen catalogues of sin in which several of them remind us that those who do such things will not enter the Kingdom of Heaven. (e.g. Galatians 5:19-21 & I Corinthians 6:9-11). Yet most people believe they will be in heaven even though Jesus said few will enter (Matthew 7:13-14).

Jim Denison's blog 1/17/22 quotes David Brooks in the *New York Times:* "Church membership has fallen below 50 percent. Our nation has the world's highest rate of children living in single-parent households. Only 35 percent believe moral truth is objective and absolute. 69 percent say any kind of sexual expression between two consenting adults is acceptable. 61 percent support same-sex marriage." More missionaries are coming to the U.S. than we are sending.

5. The church is God's bride as long as it is faithful to God. Do you love the church? The government can't save us, education can't save us, our military can't save us, and science can't save us. The church is our only hope. The true church will triumph! Hallaujah. As Veteran Missionary Don Jacobs has said, "The church defies description!"

Carnality too often characterizes the American church. We come out of the Sunday service and ask where should we go to eat. We give more money to the restaurant owner than we give in the Sunday morning offering. Our conversation seldom speaks of the pastor's message but rather of the ball game we plan to watch. Paul writing to Christians says, "I have often told you and tell you again even with tears, many live as enemies of the cross of Christ. Their destiny is destruction, their god is their stomach, and their glory is in their shame. Their mind is set on earthly things." (Philippians 3:18-19).

When is the last time you experienced a baptism service for a community person: a barber, mechanic, postman, nurse or hospital worker, a teacher or teacher's aide, a check-out clerk or bagger, a sales person, a homeless person or a family on welfare? The church in Acts added to their number daily those who were being saved (Acts 2:47). We need reviving: "If my people, who are called by my name will humble themselves and pray, and turn from their wicked ways, then I will hear from heaven, forgive their sin and heal that land," and their church (II Chronicles 7:14).

6. I said when I was at Smithville in the '60s I kept myself too busy and cheated my family of my time. I took myself too seriously. Early in my ministry I remember one Sunday afternoon weeping because I felt my message just didn't get through. Were my tears self-pity or tears of passion for my people? Paul says, "He never stopped warning his people, night and day with tears." (Acts 20:31). I am still learning to do my best and let the results to the Holy Spirit.

God can and will build His kingdom without me. Thank God for His mercy and forgiveness as I continue to make Jesus my first love rather than making love for His work my first love. When we place more emphasis on loving others than on loving God we are headed for burnout.

7. Trials and suffering are for our good. The two most painful times in my fifty years of pastoral ministry were when I experienced rejection at Northside in Lima and at Peace Mennonite in Florida. When God closes a door, He opens a better one. I never imagined God would call me to pastor a church near the capitol of the United States. What a complete transformation from a stuttering fearful child to a bold pastor. After Northside I became a church planter and after Peace Mennonite, we went to Cottage City/Capital Christian where the church grew from 45 to 400 with 20 nationalities. These were God's doings. Were it not for these experiences, I would not have become a church consultant or an author. You would not be reading this book. No matter what God allows to come into your life—rejection, pain, suffering—He will redeem it, if you give it to Him.

God has a purpose for all the wars, hurricanes, pandemics and suffering humanity experiences. They are to refine and purify His children. The Lord disciplines those He loves and chastens and scourges those He accepts. We are to endure hardship as discipline (Hebrews 12:6-7). We Americans think God calls us to be comfortable, He calls us to be faithful unto death. Jesus said, "Whoever wants to be my disciple must deny themselves and take up their cross daily and follow me." (Luke 9:23).

8. Live with a consciousness that God is in everything. To me, life consists of tiny miracles. Notice them! When I define miracle in that way, it means you will experience many miracles every day. The people you meet did not just happen by accident. It's God who directs your paths, your steps and your words. He knows our thoughts before we think them (Psalm 37:23 and 139:4).

9. Live with a holy fear of the Lord. Jesus said, "Do not be afraid of those who kill the body but cannot kill the soul. Rather, be afraid of the One who can destroy both soul and body in hell." (Matthew 10:28). Many messages today proclaim salvation by believing God loves you. That's true but you can't believe Him, trust and love Him and accept Him into your life unless you have a reverent fear, respect, and a repentant heart. There is no salvation without repentance. Peter reports that "God has granted the Gentiles (everyone) repentance that leads to life." (Acts 11:18).

10. Keep the first thing the first thing. If I come to the end of the day and feel I have not moved anyone closer to Jesus today then I need to ask God for forgiveness. So often I make comments as, God is so good to send us this beautiful weather, or notice the beautiful sky, or the birds, flowers, etc. Is it possible to see the snowflakes and not see God? Most people haven't thought about God today so the least we can do is to remind them that God is in everything.

My heart beats with Paul: "I have great sorrow and unceasing anguish in my heart. For I could wish that I myself were cursed and cut off from Christ for the sake of my people." (Romans 9:2-3).

11. Live with joy! "The joy of the Lord is your strength." (Nehemiah 8:10). Jesus told the disciples if they abide in Him, they will have a fruitful life and their joy will be full or complete (John 14:11). Two hundred sixteen times in the New Testament we are told Jesus is in us. In fact, the Father, Son and Holy Spirit are in us (John 14:23 & I Corinthians 3:16). Every day thank the Trinity for dwelling in you. The fruit, the result of His Spirit in us is love, joy, peace, patience, kindness, goodness, faithfulness, gentleness and self-control (Galatians 5:22-23). "Never be lacking in zeal, but keep your spiritual fervor serving the Lord. Be joyful in hope, patient in affliction, faithful in prayer. Share with the Lord's people who are in need. Practice hospitality." (Romans 12:11-13). Jesus said, out of us will continually flow rivers of life-giving water (John 7:37-39 AMP).

Let Paul's triplet in First Thessalonians 5:16 be the natural flow of your daily living: rejoice always, give thanks and pray continually. With the Holy Spirit in you, you can do it. Life can't get better than living in the experience of this verse!

12. Live with anticipation of heaven. We are strangers and aliens here (I Peter 2:11). Paul says, "I consider that our present sufferings are not worth comparing with the glory that will be revealed in us." (Romans 8:18). The Corinthians were eagerly awaiting Jesus' return (I Corinthians 1:7). When I think of my many friends who are in heaven, I can get homesick for heaven.

If we keep the faith there is a crown of righteousness, "which the Lord, the righteous judge, will award... all who have longed for his appearing." (II Timothy 4:8). We get to see Jesus, our loved ones who died in Christ, the great crowd of witnesses who lived for Jesus through history including the men and women of the Bible. No eye has seen, or ear has heard the things that God has prepared for us (I Corinthians 2:9). God will present us innocence of sin and with great joy to the Father (Jude 24). Even so come Lord Jesus!

MORE BOOKS BY

DAVID ESHLEMAN

50 Scriptural Meditations
(212pp. Masthof Press, 2021.) $12.95

75 Scriptures That Will Amaze You:
Living on a Higher Plane
(227pp. Masthof Press, 2020.) $12.95

Fierce Love: Balancing God's Love & Justice
(206pp. Masthof Press, 2019.) $12.95

God's Hall of Faith Speaks Today: Hebrews 11
(190pp. Masthof Press, 2019.) $12.95

Living With Godly Passion: Daily Readings
for Those With a Passion to Share Jesus
(378pp. index. Masthof Press, 2010.) $15.00

Soaring on Eagle's Wings:
When the Supernatural Becomes Natural
(373pp. Masthof Press, 2018.) $20.00

WWW.MASTHOF.COM